Making Steven Famous

Making Steven Famous

by

David Walker

Copyright 2011 David Walker

All rights reserved. No part of this book may be reproduced, stored, or transmitted by any means—whether auditory, graphic, mechanical, or electronic—without written permission of both publisher and author, except in the case of brief excerpts used in critical articles and reviews. Unauthorized reproduction of any part of this work is illegal and is punishable by law.

This is a work of fiction. Names, characters, places, and incidents are products of the author's imagination or are used fictitiously and are not to be construed as real. Any resemblance to actual events, locales, organizations, or persons, living or dead, is entirely coincidental.

The author may be reached at david-walker1@live.ca or www.davidgordonwalker.com.

ISBN 978-1-257-02505-3

*For Anne
Who Knows How and Why
Love Dave*

"One by one, they were all becoming shades. Better pass boldly into that other world, in the full glory of some passion, than fade and wither dismally with age."

— *Dubliners,* "The Dead"

Prologue

Some people crave the future. They don't seem to really be here, in the moment, because their hearts are already living in that longed-for day when their dreams will become reality.

Some people live in the past. They marinate themselves in fond or terrible memories, reinventing the past until it feels so much more real than the present.

I have it twice as bad as these people do, because I suffer from both problems...

*

Picture this: little Donny Love at age 4, blonde brush cut and skinny little chest, barefoot and wearing only his baggy bathing suit. It's a hot August afternoon in Hamilton, and the Love family (including 10 or 12 of the adopted family—fellow Scottish expatriates) is having a loud, jolly barbecue in the backyard.

Wee Donny is atop a turned-over garbage can, a plastic toy guitar in his hands. He strums, he croons and wails in his best Elvis impersonation, he wiggles his skinny little butt and shrills out insistently "Look at me! You guys, look at me!"

No one looks at Donny until his gyrations send him toppling off the garbage can. Then, his three-year old neighbour toddles over to share her popsicle. As Donny's sobs subside, the family returns to their conversation and steak.

*

Picture this: Donny, at 5, is frequently kept after school by Miss Donaldson because of his attempts to "take over the class with his comedy routines". Poor Miss Donaldson, the picture of decorum, is even driven to beat the air around Donny's head one day in her immense frustration. Donny gets the belt at home, but it does not quell his comic spirit.

*

Now picture this: Donny Love is 11. He and his buddies, Stevie, Tony, and Vinnie, have formed a club—the Mountain Boys. They ride around on the bikes that they have carefully modified, and their adventures include more than a few of the sort of pranks that I would now whup my own kid for doing, but they are full of the thrill of being alive and young and free. Their busy blue collar parents are not of the generation that micromanages their kids' lives. The result—pure, unadulterated childhood.

Donny, who is now wiry and wears aviator-style eyeglasses, is precariously perched on top of the Marconis' six-foot wooden fence, several of their plum tree's fruits in his hand. He crows like a rooster, thrilled with his prominence in this dangerous scenario, as old Mr. Marconi rushes angrily toward him from the tool shed, rake in hand. Giddy with laughter and victory, Donny leaps from the fence and he and his buds take off down the road on their "hogs", Donny cheekily yelling back over his shoulder at Mr. Marconi as they flee: "Fottiti!"

*

Donny is 13, and he and Stevie are starting a band. They intend to model themselves after the Rolling Stones. They are confident that they have the looks and talent, after just three months of guitar lessons at the Eric Goldman Studio of Guitar, to take it to the top. There is some slight tension, however, when they start their first rehearsal; they both want to be the lead singer. Donny is eventually persuaded by Stevie and their friends/future roadies to take on the role of lead guitar, a la Eddie Van Halen. "A guy who can shred guitar like that is a god," Donny agrees. "Just as important as the singer!" It's just as well, because Donny really can't sing, and Stevie has got the beginnings of a really warm tenor.

*

Donny is 14 and the band has got its first gig, at Melissa Southward's birthday party. Donny confidently tells everyone he knows that this is the moment that will launch them into rock'n'roll history. They are not getting paid, and they have to cram into a corner of the Southwards' rec room, but they are all high with the thrill of the moment. Donny hears the cheers and clapping of their small but enthusiastic audience as a taste of glories to come. It becomes one of the greatest memories of his life. He messes up a few chords, but he is a god, nonetheless. He even acknowledges that Steve is also a god. Donny's insecurities about their partnership finally vanish. They are going to the top together, like Eddie Van Halen and David Lee Roth, like Jimmy Page and Robert Plant.

*

Donny is 17, and the band is falling apart. Too much homework, says Steve. Plus, there are girlfriends now, and they take up a lot of a guy's attention. Donny is deeply disappointed. He calls Steve up frequently, ostensibly to talk about Calculus homework, but he slips in his trademark high-pressure sales tactics, trying to convince Steve to re-form the group. Steve doesn't budge, and the two have their first really angry argument, not speaking to each other for two weeks.

*

Here's the final picture for you: Donny is 18 and a half, with frizzy hair and slightly cooler glasses than he used to wear. He is wearing a rented tux and is sitting with his friends at Irondale's Graduation Prom. They are all buzzed on the beer they guzzled in the park before the dance, and on the thrill of the unwritten future ahead of them all.

Donny's circle of closest friends these days: Tony Valentini, Norbie Reingruber, John Pappas, and, sometimes, Steve McCartney. Secretly, Donny has not quite forgiven Steve for ending their ride on the Rock Star Express. But he can't bring himself to cut Steve out completely. Steve's just too good—at everything. The guy really has a charisma, and Donny soaks it up, like a moth flinging itself at a bright lamp.

There is a band playing, a real, adult band from the area—these guys are at least 24 or 25— and Donny is mesmerized. He dances like a maniac on the small dance floor, doing handstands, his shiny black shoes flailing dangerously close to couples dancing nearby. He is filled with the joy of the moment and allows himself to imagine his future as a brilliant rocker, his wailing guitar astounding his audiences.

His gymnastics are cut short when he hears a different voice on the mike. Steve. Singing The Beatles "She was Just Seventeen" like an old pro, as good as any singer out there. The students are going wild, crowding up to the stage, shrieking and whistling and totally hypnotized. Donny feels like his heart has stopped. He can't make himself move forward. He's in a bubble, filled with the sound of Steve's voice, and nothing else. He will later see that he was in a kind of state of shock. He will later know that it was because he had finally seen the truth, a truth that injured him deeply: Steve was great, and Donny was not. Steve had a future in that rock'n'roll dream, and Donny did not.

And then the weirdest part of the whole surreal evening. Steve finished the song, yelled something out to the audience, sprinted backstage, and was never seen again.

Really. None of them ever saw him again. He dropped off the face of the planet.

And what made it worse for Donny was that he had heard what Steve had yelled out over the deafening sounds of the audience.

"Ya just don't get it, do ya?!"

1.

An excerpt from the first Steven McCartney column:

And I've never met another man who was more charismatic than Steven. At age 23, he was travelling the Silk Road through Kazakhstan on a motorcycle, one of many dangerous and remarkable treks that he took in his lifetime. As he shot over the side of an embankment, he landed smack in the middle of a hijacking. Opium traffickers were attempting to kidnap the wife and children of a local government official as they travelled by small convoy through the rocky wilderness. There were machine guns and automatic rifles drawn on all sides, with the cracks of the opening round of fire still hanging in the cold air. Steven's bike landed right on top of the trafficker's truck, startling everyone, and killing at least one of the bandits in the process. The official's guards used the distraction to their advantage, taking out three more of the thugs and sending the rest flying.

In the midst of the chaos, Steven had seen the terrified faces of the children in the Jeep window, and had sprung into action, positioning himself between the gunmen and the vehicle.

When he saw that the tides had turned and the children were safe, he tapped gently on the window of the Jeep. The woman cautiously rolled down the window. Steven grinned at the littlest of the boys in the back seat and handed the woman something, gesturing to the lad.

It was his mother's tiny gold crucifix, hanging on a chain. Then, not being one for the limelight, Steven sped off. The pattern of his life.

The president of Kazakhstan publicly declared this mysterious Westerner to be a national hero in the fight against the tyranny of the drug lords.

The locals began to refer to him as "Clint Eastwood". Too many spaghetti westerns in the local theatre, I guess.

But I'll say this: this world sure could use a lot more Clint Eastwoods like my old buddy Steven McCartney...

*

Monday, September 8, 2007.

The leaves had just started to turn.

"Donny, Chamberlain wants you in his office right away."

"What?" I said, dazed, looking up from computer screen. I blinked. "Okay."

I'd been deep into writing my column and had been miles away when Meg had spoken to me. Meg Cleroux was standing over me now. My editor, Bob Chamberlain, had hired her as a student intern from McMaster University's Journalism School. She was very bright and had won the Lorne Freedman award for a series she'd written on turf wars in Hamilton between the rival Hell's Angels and The Banditos motorcycle gangs. Meg was really cute and fresh-faced, with a great figure, the kind of girl that I would have been hot for a few decades ago. Now, even in her tight t-shirts, she was just too young for me to get really excited about. I appreciated her the way a guy appreciates the sports car that he'll never be able to buy.

"You look like you've seen a ghost," she said.

"Yeah, a few actually." I shrugged. "Thanks Meg, I'll be right there."

She glided back to her desk just outside Bob's office.

Bob was, well, unique. Something of a throwback. Bob was 58 and gay as a jay, but he came from a generation that still thought that it was shameful to come out. So, Bob expended a great deal of energy and hot air asserting his alter ego : Macho Man. I honestly think that he modeled his work persona around J. Jonah Jameson from the old Spiderman cartoons. And if there was a good-looking woman around, Bob had to make a comment. If there was an arm-wrestling contest or an "open-beer-bottles-with-your-teeth" competition, he had supposedly been there, done that. If a straight guy had acted like that, someone would have pummelled him by now, but we all shrugged off Bob's antics. He really thought that he had us all fooled.

I forced myself toward his office. *Here we go*, I thought. *Chamberlain's going to fire me. He's been threatening to give me the boot for a month now. Says my articles are boring and uninspired, my writing "torpid".* "You're not writing with the same pizazz these days. What's got into you, Love? Problems at home? Mid-life crisis? C'mon, Love, throw me a bone here, would 'ya?"

That had been our conversation two days ago. At the door, Bob had said, in his usual metaphoric style, "Love, start producing professional copy or your ass is grass."

But Bob was right. I'd lost my desire to write, to work at the entertainment writing I'd built my career on. My "In Town" column had begun to sag. For the past three months, I'd grown bored and disinterested in covering concerts and shows. Something had changed inside me. At age 40, my life was nearing a crisis point. A slow paralysis had crept in. Not depression, although that was part of it, but something else, something deeper. If I didn't pull myself together, I'd be out of job. In the past, I could have handled that—I was younger then, there had been less at stake. I'd pulled the plug on my writing career a few times, had found other jobs, but always managed to bounce back into the writing game when my other career choices had bored me, or disappointed me. But I couldn't afford to do that now, because there was Cathy.

Cathy was pregnant, and in her second trimester. I'd never faced a wall like this before, and the pressure was getting to me.

Bob Chamberlain's office at *The Hamilton Gazette* sat at the far corner of an otherwise open-concept floor plan. Fifteen other journalists were also busy drinking coffee, hammering away at the keys on their computer keyboards. Ted Slater, the office cynic, was paring a thumbnail, staring at me, his legs crossed at the knees as if he had all the time in the day. A knowing smirk lined his face, but I ignored it. Every office has a cynic, I thought. They criticize everything and everyone: the *office dick,* as I'd come to think of him.

I knocked on Bob's door. It was partially open.

"Come in," he said, without looking up from his newspaper. His face was buried in the sports section of the Toronto Star. Perhaps he wasn't a fan of his own newspaper, I thought. Or perhaps he longed to work for a bigger city rag. But the sports section was definitely a ruse set up for my benefit.

He had the phone stuck to one ear, nodding. "Different, huh? A new direction for the paper?

You've had some interesting response. A few emails and letters? Phonecalls, too? Interesting, very interesting. Definitely more where that came from, Mr. Hill ..." He pretended to scan the sports page as he talked. "... Oh yes, I'm quite willing to take it to the next level. My thoughts exactly..."

To the next level? Does that mean he's going to fire me?

Allan Hill was the CEO of Hill Newspapers. He owned *The Hamilton Gazette*, as well as a bunch of Canadian newspapers and magazines. I'd never met the man. They must be planning to hire someone to take my place. Someone who would take the paper "to the next level". I was determined to get this over with as soon as possible. I could still freelance, if I had to—oh, yeah, sure, I could use the security of a regular paycheque, but not if it meant sucking up. I would never do that, not at the expense of my integrity.

Go ahead, Bob, give it your best shot.

He pointed at the door, so I closed it. He waved me into the leather chair in front of his huge, battered oak desk. I sat down and took a deep breath.

"Of course, it's all true. Donny Love is a stand-up guy. I'd trust him with my life."

My heart missed a beat.

Bob gave me a cavalier wink. His office decor, arranged by Bob himself, was a quirky mix of Ernest Hemingway and Martha Stewart. He had the walls painted a soft shade of green, with accents of pale yellow and cream around the room. I'd always found it a very pleasant room. Behind him on the walls hung several photos of fishermen with their trophies, photos of him posing with singer Celine Dionne, comedian Steve Smith, musician Tommy Hunter, actor Jim Carrey, and hockey great Paul Henderson. On his tidy desk sat a gumball machine; beside it, a portrait of himself crouching beside a bear he'd supposedly bagged while hunting last summer in British Columbia.

" ... Ciao for now."

After he'd hung up the phone, he'd feasted his eyes on one more sports detail then slammed his paper against the desk, making my heart jump into my throat.

Then his expression brightened. "Donny Love, my main man, my number one writer, my goddamn *homey,* we're going all the way on this one." Across the table, he extended a hand the size of a catcher's mitt.

Homey?

My jaw dropped. Somehow I'd expected him to hook me in the chin, not offer a congratulatory handshake. "What's this all this about, Bob?"

"Your last column shows promise, Love. Mr. Hill's received some interesting emails and letters. And you don't usually get letters, Love. Looks like people want to know more about this Steven McCartney fella. Mr. Hill likes this Steven guy, too. Likes the Clint Eastwood angle, the lone ranger of mythical proportions. And, as Alan Hill likes to say, 'always give the people what they want'."

Bob had been an editor with the *Gazette* for 10 years. He was pushing 60 years old, and last fall he'd bought himself a hair club membership. He power-lifted at Gold's Gym on Locke Street, and was perpetually in spring training mode for high school football. He loved sports, yet had a penchant for the arts, especially Broadway musicals. On weekends, he got his kicks playing touch football, but he had a season pass to the Theatre Festival down in Stratford, Ontario, where he never missed a single Shakespearean play. Bob had the build and demeanour of a steel town grunt, but his brains had given him an edge that had pushed him out of the blue collar arena into the world of academia and newspapers.

"I don't know what to say," I said, stunned by Bob's revelation. I cleared my throat.

"Listen, Love, our readership is down—The Toronto Star's more popular than ever in this town, but I think we've got something here that can put the *Gazette* on top. I think we can bring the numbers up with this "In Town" column of yours, and start putting money back in the stakeholders' hands. This paper needs an injection, and your column is the serum we're looking for! Are you with me on this, Love?" He was rubbing his fingertips together, intensity building in his eyes.

"Sure, if you think it's legal. I mean, we won't get sued for libel though, will we?"

Bob's face tightened. "Libel?" His voice became very slow and deliberate. "Only if you're lying, Love. You're not lying, are you?" His eyes bored into me.

"No, no, of course not," I said, and imagined my nose growing like Pinocchio's.

"Good," he said, exhaling long and hard. He leaned forward, his eyes widening.

"So, tell me more about this Steven guy. He actually did all his stuff ? What is he, some kinda superhero?" Bob's tone was half-respectful, half-disbelieving. "You'd better not be making this shit up, Love, or we'll be on the hook for a lawsuit. Are you making this shit up?"

"Do I look like a bullshitter, Bob?" I said, sitting up straight. *I am a bullshitter, but he doesn't have to know that. My friends know that, my wife knows that, but no one else does, and it's none of their damned business, either.*

He narrowed his eyes. "A good bullshitter never looks like one. I oughta know." He paused, rubbing his chin.

I had to get out of there—I needed to get back to my column. But first I had to satisfy my curiosity. "So, who's been calling?"

He chuckled in delight. "Mostly women from your old alma mater. That's always a good sign, eh? Appealing to the LAY-DEES."

A sickening anxiety spread from the center of my being. The office walls closed in on me. I'd done everything in my power to avoid thinking about my days as a student at Irondale Collegiate. I'd left Hamilton, or The Hammer as it's known to locals, seventeen years ago to escape the ghosts and memories and now, since April, I'd found myself back again, trying to start fresh. Revulsion lurched up inside me. Those women calling Steven had wanted nothing to do with me back in the day. But, somehow, writing about Steven had created a direct link to my past. Funny thing was that those women had wanted nothing to do with Steven then, either. But now that he was in the paper ...

Thank God Meg Cleroux was fielding the calls, I thought. She was my only line of defence. I knew, with a great sense of relief, that she also had the smarts not to give out my home telephone number.

Adrenaline was firing me up. I stood up abruptly. "Got to get back to the column, Bob. Steven's fans are waiting. And you're right—I think we've got something here."

"We're on fire!" he cried, pounding his desk again.

"On fire, Bob."

"So, when do I get to meet Steven?"

I think that the synapses in my brain actually stopped firing for a moment there.

"W-Well, that's impossible, Bob."

"Why?"

I swallowed hard. "He's dead."

Bob's mouth parted. "Oh, that's bad. Real bad. Oh well, who cares? Just keep writing that damn stuff. We're selling newspapers here, so who gives a shit? Forget dead, just write him like he's alive and kicking."

Intense relief flooded through me.

"That works for me."

I left Bob's office.

Well, maybe Steven wasn't dead, I thought, but how else was I supposed to envision someone who'd bailed on me all those years ago?

I looked over my shoulder and saw that Bob had gone back to the sports section as if we'd never had the conversation in the first place. I walked towards my desk, serenaded by the clatter of keyboards and telephones ringing off the hook.

Heads turned in my direction. Meg was on the phone, waving me towards her, leading me to believe she was fielding another phone call from one of Steven's fans. She said something into the receiver, and put the caller on hold. "Do you know a Charlene Chalmers?"

My blood curdled. The mere uttering of her name sent shockwaves through me—Charlene had been the snottiest of snotty girls. "Yeah, I went to high school with her," I snapped. Charlene Chalmers, one of the hottest, richest kids to walk the halls of Irondale, one of many who had held her nose so high it had blocked out the light. I shuddered, thinking of her. I could almost see her and her brood cackling as they hung out in the cafeteria and mocked everybody they deemed unacceptable. I saw them sneering at me, their faces hideous, ugly masks.

"I'm not here," I said, panicking, gesturing with my upturned palms, shaking my hand.

Meg rolled her eyes at me.

"She's looking for Steven," she said, "not *you*."

"Steven, of course," I said, taking my seat at the opposite desk. "Who else? No problem there. Excellent. Very good."

I stared at my tropical screen saver, heart pounding.

Meg spoke briefly with Charlene and ended the phone call. I leaned across the aisle. "Meg, please don't give out my phone number. I don't want people calling my home and bugging Cathy, you know. With the baby coming and all, she's under a lot of stress."

"I'd never do that, Donny."

"Thanks."

What the hell was I going to do, I wondered. Paranoia flew around inside me like a frightened bird.

I told myself that this would soon blow over, that the phone calls and emails were probably from a few cat-crazy women who were now desperate to hook up with someone from the past who would help them re-live their halcyon days.

The story would stay local at best, and the buzz would soon fizzle out.

But what if I'm wrong? I wondered.

Separate voices inside my head vied for attention.

Bob hasn't fired you yet, so go for it.

Yeah, but Bob's a whack job. He could suddenly change his mind about me.

Maybe, maybe not.

My wife's pregnant and I have a decent job and benefits. I'm a lucky man. I don't wanna blow it.

But what if Steven is dead? What if he died a long time ago? He hasn't called you. He must be dead. It's not really a problem if you're not actually writing about a real person.

What about libel? I'll be sued for character defamation. You can't make up shit about someone and get away with it.

Who cares? He's dead. Who's gonna sue?

I'd better care, for Cathy's sake, and the baby's sake.

The baby's not born yet. You're not hurting anybody.

Besides, Steven had wanted to be famous, dammit. He was always craving the limelight. And suddenly I realized what it was I'd been doing with that stupid column—I was forcing Fate's hand.

2.

The Steven McCartney Story, Part Two
by Donny Love

In a remote, mountain region of Afghanistan, in the early 90's, Steven made another daring rescue attempt. He'd been riding on his motorcycle through the Hindu Kush Mountains when the earthquake hit. A small tribe had been camping out beside a small river in the Bololo canyon. A young woman, dressed in a burka, had been gathering firewood at the foot of the mountain and was struggling to maintain her balance when the shaking ground upended her. Worse, the earth was splitting open. Steven had spied her from his motorcycle and had fought the shaking ground until he found that he couldn't any longer and was thrown from his bike. Undaunted, he scrambled to his feet and grabbed the woman, just as she was pitching forward into a growing chasm. When he pulled her back to safety, Mother Nature's fury hurled him into the chasm.

When he wakened, he found himself lying on a bed roll by an open fire, under a star-filled night, being nursed back to health by the tribal elders. He saw and heard things in the days and nights that followed. There were guns, a lot of them, and big crates brought in by trucks. These tribesmen were secretive, fierce warriors, but they were renowned for their loyalty, and they paid Steven much honour in the time that he was with them.

The girl who had been saved had an uncle who was very grateful to Steven. His name was Osama. Steven told me that it would be better not to ask the man's full name.

When Steven's broken bones were healed, he bowed silently to the men around the fire, and then he disappeared into the cold Afghani darkness on his bike...

3.

" ... On my way, honey," I said into the cell phone. Tonight was our first birthing class—Cathy hated to be late for anything, so she'd called to make sure I was on the way. Me, well, I'd be late for my own funeral: fact.

Driving up the escarpment in our battered 1992 Ford Tempo, I turned the radio to Hamilton's oldies station, CKOC. Marvin Gaye was singing about sexual healing. I loved AM radio; hearing the songs from the sixties transplanted me into the past, and all the streets and buildings came alive with good memories. Now I found myself remembering when Marie Hamson and I used to neck in her parents' basement. The memory tugged uncomfortably at my heart. I happened to check my rear view mirror.

Close on my tail was a black Ford Ltd. The late afternoon sun glistened in the car's grill. It resembled shark's teeth. My pulse raced a little. *An undercover cop car?* I checked the speedometer to see if I was speeding. *No, 45 klicks; no problem there.* The car pulled up beside me as if to pass, but it hesitated and slowed down, then it pulled in behind me again. Then, for no apparent reason, it dropped back out of sight behind the thickening traffic. I just wanted to get to Tim Hortons without getting a ticket.

Today's column had been a fat pile of shit. I felt as if I'd taken my first hit of crack cocaine and couldn't stop—I was hooked, instantly. Every well-crafted lie had spurred me on to write the next one. It was wrong. I hadn't been raised to lie, but I didn't care; in fact, I couldn't help myself. I'd expected to see flames shooting out of my typing fingers.

Of course, I'd done it all for Steven. I was risking my life to save his. Just once, he deserved the sweet taste of fame. At least one of us dreamers deserved to become famous. I know he would have wanted it that way. Even as I told myself this, I felt an uncomfortable twinge of conscience. Unwilling to examine my motives any more closely, I cranked up the radio.

I'd written the column wearing my old CD Walkman, sometimes listening to the *Beatles One* CD. When I was 25 and first trying to be a writer, I wrote listening to Simple Minds and Kajagoogoo, or the Thompson Twins, or Madonna. In my thirties, I'd listened to Soundgarden and Junkhouse, or even Gordon Lightfoot—if I was trying to get some of his magic Canadiana to rub off on my writing. Sometimes, if I was tired, I'd pound back the coffee and eat chocolate while listening to Green Day's *Dookie* CD, just to pump my adrenaline a little, so I could muster the energy to write. But after awhile the caffeine and sugar would wear off, and I couldn't relate to the message in the songs, so I'd go back to the age-appropriate music. Nowadays, I listen to softer stuff.

What was happening to that other guy I used to be? My confidence had started to wane in middle age.

I'd just turned off the Jolly Cut onto Concession Street, travelling eastbound along the Hamilton Mountain. I passed the park on my left, the leaves beginning to turn on the oak and elm trees. The clouds hung low in the sky like freighters that had floated off their moorings in the Hamilton Bay. When my cell phone rang, I almost jumped out of my skin. My nerves were fried. I didn't feel like answering it.

Truth was, I wasn't ready for our first birthing class at Henderson Hospital. What could I possibly do to help my wife give birth? In my dad's day, they smoked cigars in the waiting room while their wives screamed their heads off, surrounded by a bunch of strange doctors and nurses. Men today were expected to be different than their dads, and

I loved my wife and this was the new millennium and I didn't want to be an asshole about all of this. *So, let's do it, Cathy. Breathe, honey, one...two. Cathy, that's it, keep breathing...great, you're doing great.*

Someone once said that giving birth was like passing a bowling ball through your anus.

That's why you're helping your wife, Love. She's going to go through hell. Get over yourself.

The cell phone continued ringing. *Maybe it's Bob*, I thought. *Shit, better pick up.*

I took a deep breath. "Hello?"

"Love, is that you?" The voice was vaguely familiar.

"Yeah. Who is this?"

"Tony Valentini, your old buddy. Remember me, asshole?"

I held my breath for a moment. "Tony, oh my God, long time no speak! What's up?" I couldn't believe my ears.

"What's up? I read your column, buddy, that's what's up. Have you lost your freakin' mind?"

And there it was—the fatal flaw in my Steven columns: people read them. People who *knew* Steven *read* them. I had masterfully deluded myself. I decided that truthfulness was now called for.

"Yeah, if you want the truth, yes, I have lost my mind."

"Get your ass over to Tim Hortons, 'cross from the Canadian Tire at Gage and Fennel. Now!"

"What? Now? Tony, I can't. Tony I—"

"—Got no choice, buddy. Now." He hung up abruptly.

Pissed off, I threw the cell onto the passenger seat. I shook my head. *No, I don't think so, Tony. You're a ghost pretending to be Tony Valentini. But you're not him anymore because the old Tony is dead and the new Tony is someone I don't know. And you talk to me that way again and I'll kick your ass.*

You know how it is—sometimes your inner voice is a bit more macho than you could actually deliver.

Of course, everyone I'd once known in Hamilton was a ghost—I'd left this town 17 years ago, and, to be honest, I never would have believed that I would move back here with my wife, six months ago, on April 1, of all days. And, no, the irony wasn't lost on me.

I'd moved away at the age of 23 to escape— a heartbreaking first-love, ex-friends, and friends I could no longer appreciate. Down east, I had earned a journalism degree from Dalhousie University. Music had been my first love, then writing, then comedy. Instead of trying to land a full-time job at a newspaper, I'd tried my hand at writing fiction, playing in bands, and doing stand up at Yuk Yuk's comedy club. There were tons of those across Canada, so you could go to almost any major city center and get up on the stage for amateur night. When I started writing, I'd gone mostly freelance, selling my entertainment pieces to the Toronto Star, the Peterborough Herald, and the Globe and Mail. I'd met Cathy at a dance club, the Grimy Pauper, in Toronto.

Cathy was not my first love, but she became my great love. She was, I suppose, average-looking. Not a knock-out, but definitely not homely. Definitely not. In fact, when she smiled at me with adoration radiating from her, well, I was in heaven. When we met, Cathy was a virgin, and she had intended to stay that way until marriage, but she and I were naked and all over each other by the third date. It took me a couple of years to realize that I wanted to marry Cathy, and that's when she told me that she knew that I was the one after the second date. Women always seem to get these things faster than we guys do.

Cathy was like ballast for me—she smoothed out the bumps in the road and settled me a bit, without being controlling or naggy. In fact, Cathy was always my biggest supporter, in whatever I wanted to do. I had found my angel.

Three years ago, we'd married and moved into a small apartment across from the University of Toronto. I'd never felt comfortable in Toronto, but Cathy didn't want to move to Hamilton, not at first, anyway. She had a good job at the university library. With my parents aging and wrestling with various health problems, I was able to talk her into moving back to Hamilton; pregnant, she'd finally agreed.

Ever since we'd moved back here, I'd had a fear of running into people from my past.

But everyone has ghosts, Love, I thought. *You dumped friends, and they dumped you. Old band mates dumped you, and you dumped them. Get over it. Even your aging, sick parents are ghosts. Nothing stays the same.*

But if any one person had stayed the same, or almost the same, it might be Tony Valentini. Something in his voice had sounded as it had years ago.

Maybe Tony was the only old friend, other than Steven, that I might not mind getting to know again. Like everyone else from high school, we'd drifted apart. Tony had started adulthood at age twenty, when he and Angela had had a baby boy. I'd been the best man at his wedding, but then they had their second baby and he stopped calling me and I got pissed off at that, so I stopped calling him, figuring I wasn't important to him anymore, and then two years later I thought about calling him, but too much time had passed and I figured it would be really awkward. End of story.

Had we grown too far apart? Would he think I was that same mangecake who'd moved away to prove himself better than everyone else? That I'd forgotten my roots? He used to say these things to me, smirking, of course: "Too good for us, eh, Love? Gonna make something of yourself, eh? Send us a frickin' postcard, buddy. You wait and see, man. One day you'll come back." I bristled, thinking about that. On the phone Tony had sounded as pissed as he had back in the day that time when he'd been defending the Canadian Football League against the National Football League in our beer-soaked debate.

I was more than a little nervous going to meet Tony. If he gave me a hard time, I'd tell him off and get the hell out in one piece. There was always the possibility of using the birthing class as an excuse to leave—he was a dad, so he'd have to understand.

I'd thought about ringing him up months ago, but last June I'd run into an old high school friend, Brent Carlton, at the Price Chopper Food Mart, and I'd wanted to shoot myself in the head, it was so damn uncomfortable. Whatever bond there'd been between us had only existed in Grade 11 Machine Shop class. His personality seemed shrunken. Had he always been that dull and lifeless, I'd wondered. How had I not noticed? *Run for your life, Donny. Run.* And I had. First, I told a bogus lie that I had to pick up mum for a doctor's appointment, then I quickly ducked into the next aisle, picking up momentum once I was out of sight, speed-walking until I was practically running to my car.

You can't go back, a voice had said inside my head. I felt sick inside, like a loser for trying to hook up with old friends because no one else had wanted him a lifetime later. Should any of us ever be that desperate? So, after that, calling Tony had been out of the question. After my incident with Brett, I wouldn't have picked up the phone for any of my old friends, even if my life had depended on it.

4.

Get in, get the hell out, and get home in time to take Cathy to the birthing class.

The Tim Hortons sat at the front of the Plenske strip mall. There was a dollar store, a Canadian Tire hardware store and a Blockbuster video store. The mall was housed in dull brown brick. The sun dipped low in the sky, warming the brick and filling the shop windows with a red and orange glow.

As I creaked open my rusty car door, I noticed a shiny black Ford pull in to a parking spot nearby. Two solid-looking men in suits sat in front. I started, thinking back to the drive up the Jolly Cut. *Just a coincidence, Love. They're not following you. You're not that important. Besides, the whole nation is addicted to Tim's coffee. They just want their daily fix, OK?*

I prepared myself mentally to deal with seeing Tony. I had visions of him with a big gut hanging over his belt, his face ravaged by time.

Paranoia fluttered in my belly.

I struggled not to turn and run. I had to face up to my past. God knew I'd been running from it long enough.

The pressure of the two bullshit columns I'd written, plus my wife's pregnancy, was beginning to eat me up inside. What was Tony going to say about the columns?

I repeated myself in hopes of encouraging myself: *Get in, get out, and get home in time to take Cathy to the birthing class!*

Valentini will be a disappointment. You know you can't go back. Do the Brent Carlton Price Chopper shtick and run off before he can say "french cruller".

I opened the door and walked through.

"What the hell you writin' that shit for, Love? It's a bunch of lies and you know it," a male voice muttered, right into my ear. I spun around nearly jumping out of my skin.

"C'mon, I already have us a table."

I followed him, flustered, trying to get my bearings.

He hadn't turned into a bloated old geezer after all; I found myself grinning, embarrassment flushing my cheeks, suddenly glad to be visiting an old friend. I couldn't believe my eyes—Tony looked almost exactly the same, save for a few more wrinkles, and shorter hair. Greyer hair. We moved to a four-seater across from the main serving counter, next to a glass display case offering gift certificates, shiny coffee mugs, and tins of coffee. He was still wearing his grey Canadian Tire mechanic's coveralls.

We shook hands and sat down.

"Hey, man, good to see you," I said. I meant it.

"So, you came crawling back?" he asked, a wry grin eating up his face.

"Yeah, yeah, let's not go there, okay?" I shook my head. "I knew you were going to say that."

"You want a coffee?" He had one on the go on the table in front of him.

"No, I'm good, man. Cathy and I are going to a birthing class at six, so I can't stay long." I took a deep breath. "So, how's Angela?"

"She's good, yep." His gaze was unblinking.

"And life in general?"

"Same shit, different pile."

I laughed—Tony didn't mince words.

In my mind's eye, I saw Tony's eighteen-year-old self, his long curly hair jiggling on his shoulders like menacing black snakes, his juvenile tough-guy expression screwed tightly onto his face, a DuMaurier cigarette dangling from his mouth, and a cold Export beer in his hand. That was the Tony I remembered.

In a blink of an eye, he was gone. Now, in front of me, sat 40-year-old Tony, wearing coveralls darkened and splotched with oil. I nervously pre-empted the inevitable topic.

"How many kids you got, Tone?"

Tone? He must think you're an idiot. We're not in highschool anymore. Tony, not Tone.

"Four. After Frankie we had three girls. Oldest two are in university now. You?"

"One, well, almost one."

He nodded. "That's a start, but you left it a bit late, eh? You're going to have your hands full, old man."

We talked about kids and wives, the usual stuff to break the ice that had grown quite thick and crusty over the years, when, out of the corner of my eye, I saw the two businessmen from the black Ford sitting against the far window. One of them seemed to be surreptitiously looking at me.

I looked back to Tony, feeling unnerved.

"Love, you alright? You look like you've seen a ghost."

"No, I'm cool."

Cool? No, you're not, that's a lie.

Anxiety rose inside me. Clearly, I was getting neurotic.

Even the grease rimming Tony's fingernails was starting to freak me out.

"Let's cut the bullshit, Love. We go way back, remember? It's good to see you and all, don't get me wrong, but I've been reading your column and I think you're digging yourself a pretty deep shit hole. I also think you're a little frickin' nuts." He punctuated his last statement with a loud slurp of his coffee.

"Yeah, is that what you think?" A mysterious anger rose up inside me and tried to punch its way out. "You think that Steven didn't deserve to be famous?"

Tony's brow creased. "What's that got to do with anything?"

"You know exactly what I mean. You saw what Steven was capable of back in the day. You saw his potential."

"Potential? What, so the guy did the ventriloquist dummy act at the variety night every year and he deserved to be famous? Yeah, right. Whoop-dee-do." He smirked.

I felt a jolt of pleasure. "Hey, I'd forgotten about that! You're right, he was excellent at that, too."

Tony gave a half-shrug."Okay, he was good at that. So, what high school in Hamilton or anywhere else, for that matter, didn't have some kid who was going to be the next big thing?"

"Yeah, but you remember how good he was at the grad dance that night? He blew us away. Listen, Tony, I've played in bands and I've made studying the music scene my life and I can tell you, Steven had what it takes to make it in music or show biz or whatever the hell he wanted. The guy was pure fucking genius."

I realized he wasn't listening. I'd caught him with his eyes wandering, but he flicked his gaze back to me before I could see where he was looking. "Love, you remember that old fifties game show, *This is Your Life?*"

"Yeah?"

He shifted his gaze past my head. "Well, buddy, this is *your* fucking life."

I followed his gaze. Outside, on the way in were what appeared to me at first to be bizarre distortions of the two other friends we'd hung out with in high school.

"You didn't tell me *they* were coming here!" I whispered, annoyed.

"Would you have come?"

"Probably not," I muttered, shaking my head. This was all becoming way too much.

Tony leaned across the table and whispered: "Pappas is alright, but Reingruber's gone a little weirder since you knew him. Two years ago, he was charged with arson. Said he didn't do it—a good lawyer got him off. Reingruber always said that it was mistaken identity. But we don't talk about that, okay? It's an unspoken rule. Obviously, the guy's a fucking nut ... but other than that, he's not half bad, same old Norby."

I stared at Tony, stunned by his revelation. My jaw had dropped. *Who are these people? Reingruber's an arsonist? What in God's name am I doing here? What's Pappas? A serial killer?* A shudder ran down my spine. Being here felt wrong. I shouldn't have come. I should have gone straight home. I had to get out of here as fast as possible.

John Pappas strode towards us first. He extended his hand. His face was still as cherubic as ever, almost pre-pubescent. He looked as if he'd somehow reversed the aging process. "Hey, Donny. Read your Steven article. Outlandish pack of lies, of course, but I do like the feel of it. Welcome back to The Hammer, man."

One thing that hadn't changed about John was his smooth voice, like molasses dripping off a spoon, sweet and slow. Somehow he managed to sound both smart and stupid at the same time. A pair of narrow-fitting beige slacks hugged his legs, which were long and lean like a dancer's, and under a waist-length black leather coat he wore a black turtle neck. A pair of polished black leather shoes, skinny at the toe, stuck out from his legs. He was an outlandish, bohemian presence in the Tim Hortons.

He slid into a seat at our table.

And there, plunking himself down right beside me, was Norbert Reingruber, or Eggie, as John had called him back in the day. He had an egg-shaped head, a thick neck, and a big puffy face with a greasy elfin beard, matted at the ends, and he was stroking it to a fine point with his pudgy fingers. I'd expected him to stink of BO, but he didn't. In fact, he smelled quite nice— some kind of cologne. A black leather vest with a Harley Davidson logo on the back hugged his belly, and he wore a faded blue Led Zeppelin t-shirt. I could picture him on the first day of Grade 3, wearing the lederhosen that his immigrant mama had innocently put him in. I blinked away the image. He had a glazed look in his eyes.

My thoughts naturally took a turn to the cynical. *Good to be back in The Hammer. Back with the losers who never left. A loser back to hang with the losers he left behind. Living in the land of the losers has never felt better. If Tim Horton were alive, he'd be very proud to host this reunion at his donut shop.*

I pasted a smile on my face and we shook hands. He had a limp grip.

"So Norb, what are you doing these days?"

His tenor voice sounded thick and slurry, as if he'd taken too many hits to the head. "Not much, you know, working part time at Talbot's Trading Card Shop."

"Yeah?"

"Yeah, yeah, been working there on and off for 10 years, anyway."

He looked at the others for verification.

"Yeah," said Valentini, "about 10 years, Norb."

"Easily 10," said Pappas. "10 solid years." One eyebrow had gone up.

"Where you living, Norb?"

"Still living with Mom," he said, "but in the basement. I turned it into an apartment. Got my own entrance now."

"Cool," I said. *Oh, God. This is just pathetic.* "I thought you used to work at Dofasco." Dofasco was one of Hamilton's largest steel factories.

Valentini kicked me and gave me a dirty look. I figured not working there anymore had something to do with his arson allegations. "Norb, can I buy you a coffee?"

"Sure, bud. Make'er a 4X4, if you don't mind. Four creams, four sugars."

"Large black," said Pappas.

"I'll buy," said Valentini, "Love, what do you want?"

"Large double double."

As Tony went for the coffees, we three sat and stared at each other, smiling awkwardly, nodding, not quite knowing how to proceed next. *You can't go back*, my internal voice nagged smugly.

"Wow, so guys, what the hell's new?" My voice sounded an octave higher than usual to my ears.

They nodded, as if I'd asked a rhetorical question.

"Long time," Pappas said.

"Really long," Reingruber said, staring at me, a greasy smile lighting up his face.

Yikes.

"Now, the last time I saw you guys was at the McDonald's at the corner of Mohawk Street and Upper Gage Avenue, about two months after the Prom. Remember, we hooked up for lunch and then drank a twelve pack in my parents' basement?"

Puzzled expressions crossed their faces.

Pappas shrugged. He hadn't gained more than a pound since high school. He was still a handsome man. It was incongruous, him sitting beside Reingruber. Like Legolas and Gimley, for God's sake.

"Okay, so you guys don't remember that. John, what are you doing these days?"

"Still running the restaurant. It's one hell of an exciting career." He was still as sarcastic as ever, apparently.

"Really, after all these years? Wow, I'm blown away. I haven't held a job longer than a year." Even as I said it, I wished that I hadn't.

Pappas' well-groomed eyebrows rose. "Why not?"

"I dunno," I said, evasively. This conversation was seriously uncomfortable.

"We've got awhile. Spill." He draped an arm over the back of his chair.

"Some other time."

"Well," said Pappas, "don't feel so bad. At least you're not a loser living in his mom's basement." He snorted appreciatively at his own joke.

"It's an apartment, dickhead," Reingruber said, with an odd calm. "And I pay rent."

Pappas was grinning. This kind of good-natured baiting had always been part of their pattern.

"Still have that comic book collection?" I asked Norbert.

"10,000 strong and still rockin'," he stated proudly.

"You're such a fucking loser," Pappas said. "You're 40 and you're living with your mom *and* you collect comic books."

Reingruber knit his eyebrows together. "Yeah, well at least I'm not a poser, Mr. *GQ*."

"At least I can get laid."

"Keep it cool, boys," Valentini said in a grim tone, returning with a tray of coffees and a box of donuts. "Let's try and give Love here the impression that we did alright with our lives okay?" He set down the four coffees.

"So, you three have been hanging out since high school?" I said. "I mean, I think that's pretty amazing."

"No, it's not, it's fucking pathetic, straight up," said Valentini. "I should have moved out of this shit hole town years ago. All I'm left with now is a sore back and these two knuckleheads." He rolled his eyes and drank some coffee.

"Your article, Donny," Pappas said, drily, "not bad, bud. Very entertaining. But how do you plan to crawl out of that shit heap?"

"With a big spoon," Reingruber said, chortling at his own joke.

Norbert just wasn't the brightest bulb on the porch, never had been, but he'd tagged along with us back in the day, and we'd all felt a little dumped by the popular clique in high school, so we couldn't quite bring ourselves to do the same to Norbert. He was always there when we needed an extra guy for road hockey. The thing that made him likeable enough was his awesome comic book collection and his illustrations; that part of his brain actually had a brain, if you know what I mean. Truthfully, though, Reingruber did have some smarts; it's just that he always made himself look stupid. That was my theory, anyway.

We're all retarded adolescents, I thought, thinking back to Reingruber's joke. I couldn't hold a job, Pappas acted like he was still chucking spitballs at Reingruber in Grade 10 History class, Reingruber was living with his mom in her basement, conjuring up arsonist fantasies, and Tony Valentini ... well, what about Tony? Where did he fit in on the scale of mental retardation?

Tony, the Grand Inquisitor, stared at me pointedly. "You're a meatball, Donny. It's *you* who wants to be famous; you don't care about making Steven famous. Isn't that right?"

My stomach flipped over and I felt hot blood rushing to my face.

The others looked at me questioningly. A rim of icing sugar lined the top of Reingruber's mouth.

Awkward silence. I decided to deflect this painful conversation.

"C'mon Tony, be honest with yourself. *You* wouldn't mind being famous for a while. You know you'd love the attention, the flashing lights, the dough. Who here wouldn't mind the dough? Pay off your house, maybe. Quit your day job. And after awhile, the fame fades away and you're set for life and the media leaves you alone."

"Well, when you put it that way," Tony said, chomping on a sour cream glazed donut.

"I'd love to be famous," murmured Reingruber, his big face all dreamy. "Think of all the chicks you could score. They'd be all over you." I had a sudden mental image of Reingruber out on a date with a lovely girl who shared his interest in sunset strolls on the beach, romantic dinners by candlelight, and snuggling up by a big cozy fire, perhaps one Norb had set in an old warehouse, or a dumpster.

Pappas was grinning. "I should've gone to La-La Land. A guy like me could go far in Hollywood. I'm a triple threat, man—I can sing, act, dance. Gene Kelly in the 21st century!"

"Dancing is for queers, Pappas," Reingruber snorted.

Pappas gazed at him with condescending pity. "You know nothing, Eggie. Women *love* men who dance. It turns them on. Haven't you ever watched salsa dancing or the tango? Man, it's practically sex on the dancefloor."

Reingruber's brain was working hard to re-evaluate this new information. I had another unbidden mental image, this time of Norbert in tight black pants and a white buccaneer's shirt, unbuttoned to the navel, while he salsa danced with some hot Latina. It was alarming.

Pappas turned his attention to Tony. "Well, what about you, Tony? Any burning desire to be famous?"

"A grease-monkey wop from Hamilton? Famous?" Tony snorted, then paused uncomfortably. "Well, I wouldn't mind being a famous race car driver. But I'd only drive Indy 500. I'm not interested in any of that Hollywood bullshit. Boys, just give me a race car and a shot at the Indy and I could die at peace knowing I'd had that one shot." He rapped the table with his knuckles. "Win or lose."

"Well, what about Steven?" I said, balling up my resolve. "Don't you think he deserves to be famous?"

"Steven's dead, Donny," Pappas said.

"That's never been confirmed," Tony jumped in.

"*I* thought he was dead," Reingruber added.

"Well, of *course* he's dead," I said. "What else? I mean, no phone calls, no letters, no nothing. A guy doesn't just decide to abandon everybody." *Except for me, apparently.* "I mean, he has to be dead." My voice had a hint of a tremor in it. "John, who told you he was dead?"

"Reingruber. Right, Norb, you said you heard it from Dale Richardson over at Cactus Jack's bar. You said that Dale said that Steven had been killed in a hunting accident up in Smith's Falls."

"Well, I was pretty loaded, but that's what I think I remember."

The journalist in me was getting a bit annoyed with this broken-telephone shtick. "So, did you see his name in the obituary section in the *Gazette*?"

They all traded glances and shrugged.

I found myself staring at the suited men by the far window. They were stone-faced, staring past us. There was something intelligent and predatory in their demeanour. In front of them sat empty coffee cups. It pissed me off seeing them there. They're some kind of agents, I suddenly thought with alarm.

"What's wrong?" said Reingruber. His bushy eyebrows made me think of a quizzical dog.

I went for it. "I think I'm being followed," I muttered.

I looked back at Tony and motioned with my head towards the men. I leaned across the table. "I'm being followed by cops or something. I think my column has sparked some kind of investigation." Even as I said it, I knew that it was a ridiculous idea. I was a nobody. No one would take my column seriously. It was laughable, really.

Tony looked over at them, smirking, then back at me. His expression had changed. He spoke quietly. "Shit. It sounds crazy, but could swear that I just saw one of them muttering into his sleeve. What the hell kind of trouble have you gotten yourself into, man?" He glanced back at them surreptitiously.

Panicking, I knocked my coffee and it sloshed over the sides onto the table and started dripping onto the floor. "Shit!"

I grabbed some napkins out of the metal dispenser and started wiping up the mess. I noticed the time on my watch, and alarm bells sounded in my ears. "Shit, I'm late for the birthing class! Cathy will freak. I've gotta run. Catch you guys later!" I jumped up and raced for the door. "Thanks for the coffee! Nice to see ya again!"

Get in, get out. Yeah, right. You blew it, Love!

I burst out the door.

The Agents uncoiled and headed out the other door, managing to slide along calmly at an alarming pace.

But those bastards wouldn't get a hold of me. I had a birthing class to attend. And an old friend to make famous. Nothing would stop me.

Nothing.

5.

"… Breathe, honey, that's it. You're doing great. In one, out one. Pfff, Pfff."

All at once, an older father-to-be beside me, Bill, started coughing. He was a tall man in his early fifties, his wife in her early thirties. What had started out as coughing became strident hacking; on from there, thundering, nerve-wracking horfing sounds. Everyone stopped and watched Bill; expectant fathers sat back on their haunches and wives lying down on black mats watched in full shock at the Bill Show. Bill's face was turning the colour of a juicy red tomato. The veins in his temples bulged. His jerking motions tipped a pack of Export Plain filterless smokes out of his breast pocket.

"Are you okay, Bill?" I asked. "Can I get you some water?"

Cathy nudged me—she heard the trace of hilarity in my voice; she knew me all too well.

Bill's wife was as red in the face as her husband. She wasn't sure where to look. She vainly smacked him on the back.

Everyone kept staring. The birthing class facilitator, a petite woman in her forties with blonde hair pulled back in a pony tail, had retrieved some Kleenex and was handing it over to Bill. She was a nurse, and was doing her best to remain calm, despite Bill's outlandish coughing fit. Some of the women in the room looked nauseated by the phlegmy sounds coming from the poor guy.

After awhile I couldn't help myself and started to snort. The entire episode struck me as ludicrous. I tried to hide it behind the back of my hand, as if I were trying to wipe off a crumb of food from the corner of my mouth, but Bill was getting worse with each passing second. If this kept up, he was going to have an aneurism, and someone would have to plant their lips on him and give him mouth-to-mouth.

Cathy sat up on her mat. She fixed her eyes on me in warning and muttered angrily, "You made us late, dammit. You're always late. Why can't you take anything seriously, Donny? Just grow up?"

I glanced nervously at the others, to see if they had overheard her. Thankfully, they were too taken up with Bill's drama.

I thought: how can you take a man with a huge head hacking his lungs out seriously? Especially at a birthing class. It was funny. I mean, this was supposed to be a serious class, and I was trying to do the right thing and be supportive, but not with Bill hacking his liver out of his maw. I couldn't just pretend not to find things like that funny. I suppose the proper thing to do would have been to laugh about it afterwards in the car with Cathy. Anyway, at that point, I knew that the best thing to do was to shut my mouth.

With slow, stiff movements, his wife heaved onto her feet. She was at least eight months pregnant, about the same amount as Cathy. She helped Bill to his feet. His face was turning purple.

"I think it was the spices in the chicken wings," she said apologetically over her shoulder, as she took the tissue box that the facilitator gave her. "We ate suicide wings before we came here."

We all nodded to show our support, because that's what you're supposed to do when you're attending a birthing class: show empathy. Or, in my case, try to discover it. I mean, you couldn't be expecting a baby and not be empathetic, right? So obviously I needed to get on board with the empathy deal. But I'd laughed at Bill: unforgiveable. I made a pathetic attempt to redeem myself by leaping to my feet and holding the door open for him.

Bill's wife smiled at me gratefully. I felt I could really get good at the empathy thing. Then I felt Cathy's piercing gaze. *She* wasn't fooled.

There was an awkward silence.

"Okay," our facilitator said, all chirpy again. "Everyone back to their positions. "Breeeath. In and out. C'mon now, that's it ... "

Pfff, pfff ... "

6.

The Steven McCartney Story, Part Three
by Donny Love

Steven was nineteen when he found himself in Mesa Verda National Park, in Colorado, a place both spiritually and physically connected to Chaco, New Mexico. He'd been booting up more than 7000 feet of desert on his vintage brown ACE motorcycle, when, from a distance, he spotted an archaeologist giving a guided tour to a group of hot and tired hikers. He leaned his bike against a rock and caught up with the tour group. Steven had always been fascinated by ancient peoples and he quickly fell in with the group. As they stood on one of the ruined walls, admiring the ancient masonry work and the stone towers of the ancient Anasazi, Steven began to chat with a man by the name of Ethan Coen. Coen was taking photographs of the ruins. Steven, sensing that this man was somehow different, asked what he did for a living. Coen was a budding film editor who was also writing screenplays intended for Hollywood. Whether it was the hot sun beating down on his head, or the ancient Indian spirits working through him, a story idea blazed through Steven's head. He quickly jotted down the plot idea and handed it to a bewildered Coen. Exhausted, Coen had plunked himself down in the shade to mop his brow. As Steven leapt gracefully onto his ACE, his parting words were: "This is no country for you, old man!"

7.

Tuesday, Sept. 9.
10:00 p.m.

I'd called Valentini and asked him to round up the troops and bring them to Tim Hortons. He'd made a fuss about the time of night and having to get up for work and all, but he said he'd make the effort. I'd said that I had an important announcement to make. He said that the only important announcement he'd ever heard in his life had been when the Edmonton Oilers Hockey Club had announced they were trading Wayne Gretzky to the L.A.Kings.

We found a table next to the one we'd sat at two days earlier.

I licked my lips and started right in. "I need your help, guys."

"Yeah?" said Tony, folding his thick fingers on his stomach. He was dressed in his civies now, jeans and plain blue t-shirt. A big, sarcastic grin lifted the corners of his mouth. "What kind of help, Donny?"

I leaned forward and cradled my coffee cup. I heard Cathy's disapproval ringing in my ears: *"you're late, you're always late, you'll be late for your own funeral, why are you always late?"*

"I can't make Steven famous on my own," I said, "I'm going to need everyone's help."

A chilly calm settled over me. I had chosen my path at the fork in the road, and all that was left now was to follow it.

"Help?" said Pappas. "After that article you wrote in today's paper you'll need a lawyer's help, buddy. Steven gave Ethan Coen his story idea, eh?" He chortled.

"I'd give him 20 years hard time," said Reingruber, laughing through a mouthful of sour cream donut. He had a healthy appetite, Norb did.

I'd give you a 100 years, you freaky bastard arsonist boy.

"Listen," I said, forging ahead desperately, "forget what I wrote. Let's do it for Steven. Whatever it takes, let's make him famous. Dead or alive, let's do it for Steven. He was the most talented guy we've ever met, or will meet again, and, trust me, I've met tons of showbiz people over the years (*half-lie*) and he puts most of them to shame."

"I'm not going to make shit up about Steven and end up in jail," Tony said. "Anyway, I still think this is really all about *you*, man."

"Who said anything about going to jail?" I said, ignoring his last comment.

"Well, you'll be going, that's for sure," he said, laughing, darkly. "Character defamation, slander, and I'm sure we'll add impersonation, as well, once you start dressing and acting like

Steven so you can become famous you obsessive idiot." He shook his head at me.

"Don't worry about me."

"Well, I don't know if Steven wrote any screenplays, but I think he must have been a pretty good stand-up comic," said Reinbruber. His high, reedy voice reminded me of The Godfather. I myself witnessed Steven performing at Yuk Yuk's back in the day."

"No, you didn't, did you?" said Pappas.

A sheepish grin spread across Reingruber's face. "Sometimes I used to follow him around and take pictures of him."

"What the fuck?" said Tony, staring in disbelief. "Norbie, you really are a freakin' weirdo!"

Reingruber nodded as if he'd just been complimented on his geeky taste in comic book T-shirts.

My stomach sank. *Who are these freaks? And, for the thousandth time, what am I doing here?*

Reingruber stroked his beard, grinning, staring down at the table. "Well, I was jealous of Steven then, you know, because he was so funny and talented, and I was pretty much a fat nobody, and I thought if I could follow him, I'd figure out how he did his thing and maybe I could get a piece of that." He sighed heavily, reached into his pocket, and pulled out a handful of photographs. He dropped them on the table.

"Whoa," Pappas said, laughing with the same mocking tone he'd used against Reingruber in high school. "You're such a freak, Eggie. I can't believe you stalked Steven."

"Don't call me Eggie," Reingruber said, through gritted teeth, uncharacteristically angry. "I'll fucking drive you the next time you say that."

"Un-freaking-believable," Tony said, stiffening in his chair.

I snatched up the photos, and spread them open like old hockey cards. "Jesus, there he is," I whispered, reverently.

There were photos of Steven getting into his old beige Mercury Bobcat, backing out of his parents' driveway, walking out of Mike's Submarines carrying a sub and a chocolate milk, and one of him entering the front door of Yuk Yuk's comedy club on downtown John Street. Another showed Steven up on the stage, the crowd in their seats buckled over with laughter.

That was the "portal to celebrity" that Steven had joked about, and there it was, on celluloid, Steven walking into the mouth of the portal, and succeeding. He wasn't someone whose talents and potential I'd let my mind exaggerate over time. Steven had been that comic genius, and the proof was in that last picture! He had not missed his once-in-a-lifetime chance to go through that portal to greatness.

Shivers ran up and down my back, filtered into the backs of my thighs. I felt as if I'd just held the Holy Grail. I looked up and noticed that Pappas and Valentini were just as in awe as I was.

Reingruber looked sad.

"Are you okay?" I asked.

"I miss Steven."

I thought he was going to cry.

We fell into a deep silence, dissolving into the past.

A blinding flash of light stunned me. Movement. A machine-gun fire of photographer's flashes from some guy who'd been drinking coffee only a few tables away. He shot a few more of me, backing away as he did, then turned and fled.

"Who the fuck are you?" Valentini yelled, getting to his feet.

"Hey, what the hell do you think you're doing?" I said, simultaneously.

Valentini lunged, but the guy dodged his advance and flew past him out the far exit door, his coat flapping against the closing door.

"That was weird," said Reingruber, calmly.

We were on our feet, staring at the guy, who was now crossing Fennel Avenue and hopping into his car at the 24-hour supermarket across the street. Even at that late hour, the parking lot was busy with cars and he disappeared behind the building.

Slowly, we took our seats again. The Tim Hortons ladies behind the counter were staring at us nervously.

A smirk grew on Pappas' face. "*Making Donny Famous*. Ever considered naming your column *that*?"

"Very funny, Papsmear."

Momentarily, I'd regressed back to high school.

"Oooh, good one, Donny, good one. Nice and juvenile."

At first, Pappas had kept that part of himself hidden, and so had I, but underneath he was still the same sarcastic bastard he'd always been, and so was I. At that moment, I didn't know whether to hug him or hate him.

"Why would someone be taking my picture?" I said, shifting my gaze around the room, suddenly remembering two men watching me the day before.

But I knew the answer as soon as I'd said it; it had something to do with my columns. Either someone I'd lied about had read it and was building a lawsuit against me, or some mysterious government agency had decided that my stories hit a little too close to home. Maybe I was to be eliminated! I shuddered, then shook myself back to reality. That stack of suspense thrillers on my bedside table had apparently infected my brain!

I sighed.

"How do you know that wasn't Steven taking the pictures?" Valentini asked, half-jokingly. "He was like that, you know. He was always one step ahead of the punch line. I wouldn't put it past him."

"I hope it *was* him," I said. "At least I could trust *him* with the pictures."

"He did have excellent comedic timing," Pappas said.

"Fucking right it's him," Reingruber said, chomping down on another donut. "It was as if he came back to take pictures of me to get back at me taking pictures of him." The light in his eyes flickered, then died out. He saw us staring at him. "Whatever, man." And he went back to eating his donut.

Seeing Reingruber like that, I didn't know whether to laugh at him or cry for him, but what I did know was that my life was changing in ways I never could have predicted.

8.

And my columns were changing in ways I couldn't have predicted, too. I found myself writing increasingly far-fetched stories about Steven.

Column Four featured Steven rescuing several dogs from a California home during a famous rash of wild fires. I never actually came out and said that it was Pam Anderson's home, but I think that my reference to a "platinum blonde Canadian bombshell with world famous breasts" may have been enough.

Column Five featured our hero Steven single-handedly foiling a pre-911 terrorist attack targeting the Golden Gate Bridge. Apparently Steven had acquired remarkable bomb dismantling skills during his many travels over the years in the Middle East.

I guess I shouldn't have been surprised that our local news media took note. CKOC radio began station identification jingles that sang out "Home of Steven McCartney!" Our local television news station, CHCH, ran a short but excited entertainment news piece about the mysterious Steven at the end of one broadcast.

I guess I shouldn't have been surprised.

But I was.

Dumb ass.

9.

Friday, September 12.
10:30 p.m.

Offices of the world's biggest Hollywood entertainment news show, *Hollywood Tonight*.

The haggard faces around the table said it all. This production meeting had gone on for hours, and no one had had any good ideas. Producer Lou Goldberg looked like he was about to eat one of his assistants' livers with a nice Chianti.

"I fuckin' pay you assholes to come up with some goddamned decent story ideas! I swear I'm gonna' fire the whole fucking lot of you if you don't come up with a story in the next three minutes!"

From the far end of the table came a meek Cindy-Lou-Who voice. The newest assistant producer, one of a long and rapidly changing series of employees, was grabbing the bull by the horns. She cleared her throat nervously.

"Excuse me, sir, but my roommate from Canada has been talking non-stop about this mysterious, handsome hero dude from Hamilton, Ontario. They're saying that he befriended Osama Bin Laden and even stopped a terrorist attack on the Golden Gate Bridge."

"What the fuck kind of shit is this? Who the hell watches an entertainment show for political shit like that?" Lou Goldberg's recently inserted plugs were increasingly obvious as his face grew redder with annoyance. "And who the hell cares about any goddam Canadians. Fuckin' socialists??"

"Also, apparently he rescued Pam Anderson's dogs from a wild fire," she added hopefully.

Goldberg's bushy eyebrows practically went up onto his big bald head.

"Why the fuck didn't you say so? Pam Anderson is hot these days. Let's go with this, people. I want to see the romance angle—Pammy's mysterious new boyfriend. And, let's get some photos. But if he's an ugly bastard, I want Editing to do a major Photoshop on this fucker. And let's minimize the Canadian thing, right? Let them *think* he's American, just don't be too clear."

There was a gentle sigh of relief from the beleaguered assistants around the table.

Their asses were safe for another day.

10.

Monday, September 15.

"I'm not going to live like this anymore," Cathy said.

Dread spread out from my inner core. I'd just returned with milk from the convenience store, and there she was, standing in the hallway, wearing her housecoat, her arms folded across her chest. I'd dropped her off at the house after our latest birthing class—she hadn't spoken to me since leaving the class. The damp wood smell of our old house permeated my nose.

"Live like what?" I asked nervously.

"Do you know how much you have embarrassed me at these classes?"

"I'm sorry, you're right." I tried to give her a hug, but she stepped back, her gaze angry and resolute.

"You treat the whole thing like a big joke," she said. "Like it's all about you, the Donny Love Show, starring the one and only Donny Love."

I'd never seen her so intense before.

"I can't help it, Cathy. Like that smoke guy last week—he was way too funny!"

Cathy's eyes bored into mine.

"Didn't you find the situation funny?" I tried hopefully as I hung up my coat in the closet by the door.

"You're 40, Donny. It's time you learned to control yourself, if not for your own sake, then for mine." Her face was creased with anger and concern.

I felt defeated. "It's late, Cath. Let's get some sleep, and talk about this in the morning."

"There's no time for sleep, Donny. There are 29 voice mails and the phone keeps ringing off the hook! Apparently, everyone from old girlfriends to Hollywood reporters wants to talk to you, now that you're famous, Donny. You're basically down at that newspaper re-writing your own life script, and it's selling. Your big lies! What a laugh! For years you've sent your stories and manuscripts to every publisher and agent in the publishing and film business with absolutely no success, but now you're making it big, without an agent, or movie, or payment. But you're going to end up in jail for character defamation, and we'll lose the house, and this time, make it move number eight, I'll have to move out by myself because you'll be in prison, you damned fool!" She fought back the bitterness that had risen in her voice and her eyes were brimming.

"29 voice mails?" *That's too many. This is moving way too fast.*

"Who cares how many?" she said, moving closer to me. She gently poked her finger into my chest. "*You've* got a problem, Donny. *You* need help. We keep moving because you don't feel any city or town is right for you. You say you came here to help your parents, but you really came here for more than just that, Donny Love. You're trying to find something, but what? Think about it, Donny. You're never satisfied with your life even after almost twenty years of searching and changing and uprooting." She took me by the hands. "Donny, the past is dead, all *those* good times are over, but there's still a future, a *good* one. We'll have it, together." Her tone was pleading.

"I know," I said. "I know." But I didn't, not really.

The phone started to ring. I made for the kitchen, but she held me back. "NO!" She looked frightened; she was obviously afraid this mayhem I'd created was going to destroy us.

"You're right, I have to get a grip on myself."

She lowered her voice. "Look around you, Donny. There are packing boxes still unopened. You've been promising to unpack them now for six months. Deep down, are you already planning your next move, your next job? Your next shot at fame and fortune? What are you afraid of, Donny? What is going on?" She'd settled her hands on my chest. Burning guilt filled my gut.

I really wasn't sure, but I did know that something *was* wrong with me, something deep inside of me that needed to be exorcised: a gibbering demon.

I gathered myself together for Cathy's sake. Her soft face looked so pained. "Listen Cathy, I know I've changed jobs a lot, and I've been searching for something since we met, but I've always landed us back on our feet. Look, we live in a nice house, finally. We're having a baby. And I promise I won't laugh out loud at the next birthing class. And I won't be late." I felt like an alcoholic promising there'd be no more relapses.

She offered a weak smile. "I wish I could believe you."

I put my hands on her shoulders. "I promise we won't move again. I'll stay with the *Gazette*, and I'll put an end to those Steven articles. Right now."

"Where did those articles come from, Donny? It's so strange. I mean, you hardly ever mentioned Steve McCartney before these columns started."

"I know, but he was a good friend of mine. And when I came here I started thinking about him again. He was the most talented person I've ever met, you know?"

I thought things were beginning to look good between us when Cathy took me completely off guard. She clamped her gaze on me, a sad and pleading gaze. "Donny, I want you to see a psychologist."

"Whoa, a psychologist? You're kidding, right?" I felt blindsided.

"I think it's time we figured out why you keep moving running from job to job, city to city."

I opened my mouth to respond but she cut me off. "I won't run with you anymore, Donny. I'm run out."

"This is about me writing, isn't it?" I pulled away from her.

"Of course it isn't. It's about *why* you write, *why* you can't settle anywhere before you get bored and depressed. Not everyone who writes has the talent to get published, Donny." She looked apologetic. "I'm sorry. I know that's a bitter pill for you to swallow."

I nodded shakily.

"Honey, this is the first full-time job you've accepted and we have a baby on the way and I can't take much more upheaval." She took a deep, pulsing breath. "Like I said, if you leave Hamilton, I'm not going with you." Tears had welled up in her eyes again.

"You sure you want me to see a psychologist?" I said, staring at a point on the living room floor. A dark depression filled me, and I wondered what the hell was truly wrong with me. The only thing I knew for sure was that I'd always had a bad case of dreameritis.

11.

Tuesday, September 16.

Driving to work the next morning was a horror show.

In fact, the show hadn't stopped since Cathy had confronted me the night before. After she'd gone to bed, I'd listened to *all* the voice messages. It had taken me two hours. Seven of them had been from old high school friends, 'likeables" as I'd thought of them, asking how I was doing, "whatever happened to Steven?" type stuff, and did I want to get together for a beer some time? The Principal of Irondale Collegiate wondering if Steven would speak at the upcoming graduation ceremony? Michelle Green, Steven's high school fantasy girl, had called, asking where Steven lived and could I call her back and give her his phone number? Jerry Simon, an assistant producer from *Hollywood Tonight,* had called wanting to interview me. It had been the worst sleep of my life—Cathy had been crying silently in the bed beside me, tossing and turning, and the messages had fired me with such fear and adrenalin that I couldn't come down far enough to sleep. I felt as if I'd been bingeing on crack all night.

But when I opened the front door to head out to the car, my stomach hit the floor.

Apparently, the Men in Black had come to pay me a visit.

"Mr. Love, my name is Agent Smith," (*You've got to be fucking kidding!*) "and this is also Agent Smith." (*I'm not kidding, these were really their names*). Badges were flashed at me.

"We are agents of the Canadian Security Intelligence Service. I'm going to have to ask you to accompany me to answer some questions. We have already contacted your employer to let him know that you'll be a little late for work today."

I was stunned. I stood there paralyzed with fear and disbelief. The words that came out of my mouth surprised me. "Bye honey, have a nice day," I called back behind me.

Cathy's muffled voice called out from the bathroom. "Shove it!"

It was going to be a wonderful day.

12.

You wouldn't believe where CSIS had its secret Hamilton offices.

The local marijuana emporium, Up in Smoke, was constantly being closed and re-opened as a result of court battles over Canada's jellyfish marijuana laws. The grubby stoned patrons out on King Street in front of the store barely batted an eyelash as the hulking agents escorted me up the narrow stairs to the offices above the dope shop.

The building was an old turn-of-the-century brick apartment with a lot of character—creaky floors, poorly insulated, and with ornate iron heating grates that let a substantial quantity of dope smoke up into the office.

I found myself surprisingly relaxed during the interview.

In fact, it was all pretty funny.

The agents sat facing me across a steel table. They appeared to be the same ones who had tailed me a week earlier. They were both tall, wearing crisp black blazers. They had neatly manicured hair. Highly polished black shoes poked out from the cuffs of creased black slacks. They looked as if they'd stepped off the set of the movie, *Men in Black*.

One bright light dangled above the table. The garbage can was filled with the remnants of Tim Hortons donut boxes, 7-Eleven chili dog wrappers and numerous candy bar wrappers.

Agent Smith (I'm not sure which one) spoke first. "Mr. Love, for how long have you known Steven McCartney?"

"Since grade school."

"When did you last hear from Mr. McCartney?"

"At our high school graduation prom."

He looked up from his notes and levelled a piercing gaze at me. "How can that be, Mr. Love, when your columns reveal a detailed knowledge of Mr. McCartney's activities in the last twenty years?"

Hot shame flooded my body. Suddenly my mind was clear. I knew what I had to do. I had to end this.

I swallowed nervously. My mouth felt pasty. "The thing is, none of this is true. The columns, I mean. I made it all up. I haven't talked to Steven since Grad. He might even be dead. I just wanted to … I mean, he...you know?"

I looked pleadingly at the Agents Smith. Surely they would understand. I felt a great sense of relief that I had finally come clean and this nightmare was coming to an end.

But they stared at me unblinking and impassive.

"Mr. Love, we expected you to deny your involvement with a suspected terrorist. But I think it's time that you understand the consequences of non-cooperation. Agent Smith?"

The other Agent Smith slid a manila folder across the table towards me.

Paranoia rose up inside me. *A terrorist? What could these granite-faced grim reapers have on me?*

With a shaking hand, I opened the folder. It was worse than I thought.

Four yellow parking violations, unpaid since 1985, stared up at me accusingly.

"Mr. Love, do you know what happens to people who don't pay their parking violations?" The shadow of an evil smile played at the corners of Agent Smith's mouth.

The question hung in the air, like the dope smoke wafting out of the floor vent.

Suddenly, it occurred to me that I didn't know. Why didn't I know? Did they go to jail? Did they *disappear* like Steven had disappeared?

"I'm sorry, I must have forgotten about them! H-how much do I owe you?" I started to reach for my wallet.

Agent Smith put up his hand. "That won't be necessary, Mr. Love. In fact, I think that you will find there are many *benefits* to cooperating with CSIS."

Across the steel table, he slid a Boston Cream donut on a Tim Hortons napkin.

We all eyed the donut, its icing glistening under the lamp.

It was now obvious to me that I had no choice. I had started this lie, and I was going to have to continue it because they wouldn't believe the truth.

The sad thing was that I was kind of looking forward to it.

13.

Tuesday September 16.
11:00 a.m.

"Would you like some tea, son?" Dad called, from the kitchen.

"Sure," I said. "Do you need a hand?"

After my interrogation, I couldn't face work, the questions, and the lies that I'd have to make up. Instead, I headed home on the Hamilton Street Railway bus to my parents' house. I just needed to return to old comforts.

"What?" Dad's hearing was going.

"I said, do you need a hand making the tea?"

"I'm making tea, son, not an atom bomb. It's not complicated."

"Right."

"Stop your mumbling, son."

"I said "Right" ".

"I heard you the first time, I'm not deaf, you know."

I sighed in disappointment. I'd been kidding myself, thinking that my parents were going to make everything okay. They were true Scots—they'd do anything for you, but touchy-feely was not in their genes.

"So, how's your knee, Mum?" I asked her from the recliner I'd plunked myself down in. A month earlier she'd had a knee replaced, and Cathy and I had brought my old childhood bed down from upstairs and positioned it in the middle of the living room so Mum could watch television and be close to the bathroom. The sheer curtains that covered the living room sliding doors were badly yellowed from years of cigarette smoke. Mum sat up in bed, her pink, cotton-candy hair flattened a bit from lying down.

"Achh, not too good. You know, Donny, getting old's no fun."

"Can't be easy."

She shook her head. This latest pink hair made her look like Dame Edna.

"What are you writin' that rubbish for?" Dad asked, approaching from the kitchen, his brogue thicker than the last time he spoke. Most people had no clue what my dad was saying. While my mom's accent was crisp and exact, my Dad's always sounded like he was half-way into a bottle of Drambuie.

He handed me my cup of tea.

"It's complicated, Dad."

Dad scowled."What a rubbish heap. The bing of filthy words. The nest of lies. You're writin' out your arsehole on this one, Donny. You'll be out of a job and a career if you keep it up."

"And what does Cathy think of this?" Mum piped in her sweet lilting voice. "There's a name for people who lie. Do you know what it is, Donny?"

"Mum, don't say it," I groaned.

"Donny, do you know the name for people like you? Say it out loud."

"Aw, Mum, c'mon. Please." I felt like a kid again. How did she manage to do that?

"Donny?"

I hung my head in defeat. "Okay. A bletherin' fibber."

"Aye, Donny, that's it. Now, you haven't changed much, have you?"

It occurred to me that she was right. It wasn't a very nice feeling.

Dad set his cup down on a side table, tea sloshing over the side of the cup onto the carpet, then toppled into the matching recliner beside me. Big, sputtering coughs rolled out of his mouth, and I half-expected his one remaining, cancer-free lung to hurl out as well.

Mum rolled her eyes, and chided, for the millionth time, "That'll be the death of you, Archie! Bad enough you're missing one lung and you're still smoking, you daft idiot." Her knee spasmed and she clutched it, groaning. I got up from my seat to offer some help, but she waved me down. She dragged an ice pack onto her knee and leaned back into her pillow, half-propped up. Typical Scots—they'd perform surgery on themselves if they could, rather than let someone help them.

Dad reached over to the side table, removed a pack of Export A cigs, and lit one up, mid-cough. "I'll not take orders from a woman with dolly hair!"

One of the reasons Cathy and I had moved back to Hamilton was to help my aging parents. What the hell were we thinking?

"Next thing you'll have cancer of the throat and you'll being smoking a fag through a bloody hole in your neck!" Mom said, her voice rising in pitch.

"Whisht, woman, you're haverin'! I've told you, I'll die the way I choose, not the way you want me to. If you can't have a smoke at my age, then when can ya?"

"Well, I won't be far behind you, not wi' all that second-hand smoke you've forced on me!"

"Move out then, woman. But you'll have to be carried out the door by the bletherin' fibber, wi' the shape your knees are in."

"Ahhhh," she said. "Take a hike."

I picked up the television remote, or the flicker as my parents called it, and turned on the television. Some things never change. As a kid, their constant arguing used to upset me, but now I just found it comical.

"How's your tea?" Dad asked, exhaling a massive cloud of smoke.

"Great," I said.

"Is that Norbert Reingruber?" Mom said, disbelievingly, pointing towards the television, her face scrunched up.

"Ochh, you're haverin', woman. That hair dye has damaged your brain," Dad said. "Are you referring to that wee egg-heeded boy that used to play wi' oor Donny?"

"Oh my God!" I said, spilling some hot tea over the rim, burning my fingers.

I couldn't believe it. On Channel 11 news, a reporter was interviewing Norbert Reingruber. He was sitting in his mom's basement. Reingruber was in a time warp—taped to the panelled walls was the same Ted Nugent's *Double Live Gonzo* poster he'd bought when he was sixteen, as well as Rush's *2112* poster and Led Zeppelin's *Stairway to Heaven* poster that had been there since I'd known him. The famous Raquel Welch poster was still there, too. For a Grade 8 boy, that poster had been a little piece of porno heaven.

Reingruber was dressed to the hilt. He'd feathered his hair like he'd worn it in the seventies. His gut hung over a pair of tight jeans, his flab squeezed out of a Kiss Army t-shirt, and he wore a brand new pair of vintage Adidas Rom running shoes. He was plunked down in an orange bean bag chair, happy as a boy of eight, or an arsonist pushing 40.

"Oh yes, Steven and I were very close. In fact, of all his friends I was the closest."

My jaw dropped. "Bullshit!"

My Dad growled, "Hey, watch your tongue now, Donny! I'm not too old to tan your fuckin' hide, and don't you forget that."

The Channel 11 news reporter's microphone was visible at the edge of the camera.

"Had you always known Steven would be famous?"

Reingruber sounded professorial. "I knew it as far back as Grade 3. He was always the class clown, with the comedic timing of a young Gene Wilder, perhaps. The teachers never disciplined him. They were far too amused by his jokes. In Grade 9, he played Poncho in *Man of LaBamba*, Grade 10, a character in *Sweet Charity*, Grade 11, Boo Whatsisname in *To Kill a Blackbird*, and Grade 12 he was Jesus in *Godspell*..."

The interviewer hesitated for a moment, clearly thrown off by Reingruber's stupidity. Reingruber had steepled his fingers thoughtfully.

"He must have been quite a talented actor, even in high school."

My dad hissed in disgust. "He's full of shite, that one. Livin' in his parents basement. Time that lad's mother kicked him to the curb. He'll no become a man rotting in that basement. Maybe a laggard or a wastrel, but never a man."

"Too late," Mum added crisply. "He's stunted for life, that one."

"Look at the fat on him," Dad said, pointing at the television. "He's the size of a zeppelin."

"...Grade 13 was Steven's zenith, that's when he became aware that he would ascend the heights of greatness, no matter what he did. He also put a band together with a very old friend of ours." Reingruber stroked his greasy beard.

"You must be referring to Hamilton's own Donny Love."

"Yeah, yeah, Donny. Anyway," he said, shifting in his chair, "here is my archive of photographs chronicling this important stage in Steven's rise to fame." The camera zoomed as Reingruber flipped through his photo album, revealing images of Steven from grade school up to the shots of Steven entering and leaving comedy clubs, plus photos of Steven's old writer's digs down on Barton Street. Even a Peeping Tom shot through Steven's window, showing him banging out something on his old Royal typewriter.

"I played drums in all of Steven's bands," Norbert said, dropping the photo album in the bean bag chair. He hurried over and sat behind a massive drum set that would've made Neil Peart from Rush jealous. He almost fell off, he was so excited.

"Remember John Bonham's solo in Black Dog? I can play it pound for pound, man." He started hammering the skins. One of his drumsticks flew out of his hand and landed at the feet of his mother, who was smiling at the camera from the foot of the stairs. In her hands she carried a tray of milk and cookies.

The reporter turned to face the camera to wrap it up. He looked alarmed at the racket going on behind him. He had to raise his voice to a yell. "This is Jamie Dawson reporting on the Steven McCartney phenomenon right here in the basement of Steven McCartney's best childhood friend, Norbert Reingruber!"

"Best childhood friend? I can't take anymore of this crap!" I said, jabbing at the power button.

"There was always something not right about that boy," Mom said sweetly.

"Aye, he's for the looney bin, that one," Dad said.

I had to get out.

"Well, we've got another birthing class tonight at seven," I said, walking towards the door." If I'm late, Cathy will have my head. Thanks for the tea. I'll drop by again on the weekend."

I'd only made it half-way across the living room when, beyond the large window, the scene on the street outside froze me in my tracks.

A Channel 11 News Truck pulled up against the curb, followed closely by a 'City Pulse' truck, and the CBC.

14.

Fifteen minutes later, it was Barnum and Bailey's Circus out on the front lawn.

"It's bloody madness out there!" Dad said, pacing in front of the living room window. His face flushed with anger. Madness shone brightly in his eyes. He punctuated the air with his cup, sloshing more tea onto the carpet. "They're mucking up my lawn, the bastards."

"Archie," Mom said, angrily, "you're spilling tea over my good carpet." She'd clamped her hands against the side of her face, shaking her head.

"Forget the carpet, Esme, it's the lawn I'm concerned about. I spent a fortune on it, and those television people are bloody well ruining it. I've a mind to sue the bastards." Tea was dripping off his wrist now.

Mom was straining in her bed to see what was happening. "They're coming for you, son," she said, as if announcing an alien invasion. "They're coming!"

"Move your arse out there," Dad said, "and face the paparazzi. They're ruining our grass."

"Aye, the grass," Mom said. "We spent a fortune on it."

I sighed heavily. My dad was right. I'd created this monster and I had to face it. I felt like the little boy who'd once lived here and was being told to go to school and apologize for talking back to the teacher.

I bolted for the door. Panic ate me up. What was I going to say? Anger stung me. What right did these pricks have to invade my privacy like this?

This is it, I thought. *Everyone from my past will know the true me, the lying idiot who ran away from Hamilton and came back with his tail between legs—no trophy, no best-seller novel, no hit records. All the people in high school who ignored me will now have more reason to, and they'll think even less of me than they did then.*

And I was out the door onto my parent's porch, flashbulbs blinding my eyes, a throng of reporters flooding the lawn and sticking cameras and microphones in my face. Behind them, a number of kids on bikes and skateboards had followed the trucks and were hanging out on the sidewalk, pointing, thrilled with all the excitement. The black unmarked car was parked down the road. I could see that CSIS wasn't going to be rescuing me from this.

"Can we have a few words with you, Mr. Love?" called out a hip reporter from City-TV; he looked to be all of twenty.

"Yeah, I guess so." The wall of reporters had blocked my route down the concrete walkway.

Run, run while you can!

But I couldn't. Lead had filled my legs. The wind dragged a heavy sulphurous stink across my lawn, courtesy of Dofasco.

"Are you still in contact with your old buddy Steven McCartney?"

Feeling sick inside, I knew that the truth just wouldn't do. It was just like the CSIS interrogation. I'd done such a good job of lying about Steven that now the truth would sound like a lie.

I knew I had to be very careful with this lie. "I'm in frequent contact with Steven, but on his terms and not through the usual channels." As soon as I said it, I knew it was the wrong choice of words.

The reporters jumped excitedly on that. The CBC reporter's resonant voice cut through.

"Are you saying, sir, that it is too dangerous for McCartney to use phones and email? Just what is it that Mr. McCartney is doing now that puts him at such risk?" Leave it to the CBC to cut to the chase so quickly.

My heart thumped loudly. I had to be careful now that CSIS was involved.

"Actually, last time I talked to Steven, he was working on some music, stuff like that. Nothing dangerous." I tried to sound convincing. My stomach was in my throat.

City TV piped up again. "What kind of music?" This was right up their alley, with their young urban audience.

"Well, Steven was always a fabulous singer. Just ask anyone from our high school, Irondale Collegiate. He had, I mean, *has* a fantastic pop voice. And he can mimic any male singer's voice, note for note. He was— *is* the most talented guy I've ever met. As far as I'm concerned, he's a superstar." For a moment, I'd forgotten all about the press on my parents' front lawn. I was back in my heyday, with my buddy Steven and the full potential of life ahead of us.

The excited buzz brought me back to the present. The questions came from all directions.

"What kind of music is McCartney writing?"

"Will we be seeing a CD release soon?"

"Who's producing his release?"

"Any concert dates in the area?"

"Any chance he'll be including a date at his old alma mater for their fiftieth anniversary coming up later this month?"

To be honest, I don't know how I answered the questions. I know I said yes to a couple of them, but I'm not sure which ones. And I'm not sure the reporters knew, either. All I know is that the next morning *The Hamilton Gazette* reported on its front page that super pop legend Steven McCartney was planning to make a stop on his world tour in his old home town of Hamilton. Irondale Collegiate would be proud to host his hometown debut at their Fiftieth Anniversary Concert on Thanksgiving Weekend, Saturday, October 11.

I had three weeks to find my potentially dead friend, turn him into a pop star, and present him to the world.

Three weeks.

15.

"What the hell are you doing, Donny Love?"

I was standing in the front hall, panting from trying to outmanoeuvre the news cameras standing on my front lawn. Cathy looked like Judgement Day.

"What do you mean? I just dropped in to visit my parents." I swallowed nervously as I feigned my innocence.

"How can you keep lying to me? I've been watching you on television for the past half-hour. There are clips of you on practically every station. So Steven's going to headline a big concert, is he? Steven, who might be dead. Steven, who you haven't spoken to or heard from in twenty years. You are pathetic, Donny! If you were made of wood, your nose would be twenty feet long right now!"

Cathy stormed off into the kitchen.

I felt sick to my stomach. I had visions of her leaving, dragging suitcases out the front door, and never returning.

What could I say to her?

She was right. I was pathetic.

And now there was no way I could tell her about CSIS.

16.

11:25 p.m.

Cathy and I were slumped in the basement desolately watching television.

We were watching the news, a depressing bit about the war in Iraq. The smell of our lasagne dinner was still in the air. Chocolate cake crumbs sat on the empty plates on the coffee table. Cathy had said very little to me all night after her blow-up. I couldn't blame her.

The paparazzi had clung to the sidewalk in front of our house. I'd paced back and forth in the living room while Cathy made the dinner, occasionally peering through the crack in the drapes, but every time seeing them still there. I'd called the police radio room and they'd sent around a cruiser. They'd dispersed for awhile, then returned in twos and threes until they'd amassed in original number.

I'd found myself thinking about my aging parents, wondering how life would turn out for them in the following years. I wondered what would happen to Cathy and I, wondered if, on my own, I could put a stop to my writing compulsion.

"You promised you'd paint the baby's room a week ago," Cathy said, in a grim voice.

"You're right. I'll do it tomorrow," I said, changing the channel on the remote.

"Not *the Ultimate Fighter*. It's too violent."

I changed the channel. "What do you want to watch? *Seinfeld* or *Sex in The City*?"

Cathy didn't answer. I glanced at her profile. Her eyes had teared up.

I longed to move closer to comfort her, but I didn't dare.

A flash of light through the crack in the basement room drapes startled me and I jumped up and peered through. Just headlights from the neighbour's car as he pulled out of the driveway. I scanned the street for signs of the CSIS dudes, but the street was deserted.

Cathy turned to gaze at me earnestly. "You're a nervous wreck, Donny. I want you to stop all of this. Tomorrow I want you to tell your boss the truth."

"He'll fire me, Cathy," I said, returning to the couch.

"I don't care. I just can't take the pressure, anymore. What if I miscarry?" She choked on her last word, but gained control of herself.

"It's okay—you won't miscarry. Everything will work out." It made me sick even to imagine that that could happen.

Her voice got very quiet. "The baby's due in six weeks, you haven't painted the baby's room, you haven't even tried to get in to talk to the psychologist, these entertainment people will sue you for all the lies you're telling about them, maybe you'll even end up in jail, and then you won't even know your child, and the media's stalking our house because you don't care about the baby or me." She drew in a trembling breath.

"Of course I care—"

She stared at the floor, shaking her head. A big tear dropped onto her night gown.

My mouth parted. I felt helpless to find anything to say. Numbness spread inside me. She was right. I was all talk, all lies. I was out of control. We must have sat there for a good hour, saying nothing, each passing second our marriage sinking deeper and deeper into quicksand. After awhile, desperate to break the tension, I flipped the channels until I happened on Channel 11.

My mouth unhinged all the way. On the screen was the last person I'd ever expect to see gracing the local news. He was being mobbed by reporters outside of the Canadian Tire as he rolled the giant automotive bay door shut and headed for his car in the parking lot.

Cathy said, "Is that your friend Tony?"

"Holy shit," I said.

"Steven was awesome," Valentini said. There was a weird look on his face. "We used to dream of running an Indianapolis 500 racing team one day. After high school we were going to get sponsors and Steven was going to do the promotion end of things and get the dough and I was going to start training as a driver on my uncle's dirt track out in Cayuga. He owned the thing, and I could drive on it any time I wanted. I had the talent with cars, and Steven had the brains and the chutzpah. We could have taken the racing world by storm."

"You lying bastard!" I said. "The never discussed the Indy 500 Ever. Never." I stared at his face. Now I could see what that funny look was about: guilt. Tony had been bitten by the bug and he knew it!

"How do you know they never had plans like that?" Cathy said.

"Because I just know, that's all." Jealousy rose up inside of me. My ears burned. First Reingruber, now Valentini. Steven had liked me the best, and that was that.

Cathy gave me a piercing glance. "Maybe you weren't as special to your old friend as you'd like to think," she said carefully.

"That's a load of rubbish," I said, sounding just like my old man.

Cathy's silence spoke volumes.

"You just couldn't understand the relationship between me and my old bud," I said. I crossed my arms and slumped deeper into the couch. A big, sulky kid.

I couldn't believe Tony was spilling like this. Not once had he ever shown any desire for the spotlight. In fact, he had no use for famous people, so I'd thought. I knew then, more than ever, that everyone desires to be famous, even if just a tiny bit.

The scene on the screen changed to Pappas' restaurant. *No frickin' way! I can't handle this!* John was standing there with his arms crossed, dressed in black pants, a crisp white shirt, and a thin black tie, very eighties and waiterly. He posed the same way he had in the school halls between classes. A cocky grin ate up his face. "Sure, I knew Steven back in the day. We used to chill together."

"Did you have any idea Steven would become famous?" the reporter asked.

Pappas narrowed his eyes and gave a slow dramatic nod. "Of course, I did. Truthfully, though, any one of our group could have been famous if we'd taken the risk." His voice had taken on a funny tone. "It takes a special kind of person to do that—you know, just throw it all away, walk away from everyone who loves you, all your responsibilities to people..." His voice trailed off and I saw sadness in Pappas' eyes.

The reporter apparently didn't like the way the energy was draining out of the interview, so he jumped in with the next question. "When was the last time you spoke to Steven?"

Pappas suddenly turned back on. "I had a few chances myself, you know, to have a career in the biz. I used to be able to dance like nobody's business." He saw the camera woman starting to make the wrap-it-up gesture to the reporter.

"Wait, wait, check this out!" Pappas said, and he slipped into a tap dance routine straight out of *That's Entertainment*. It was surreal. The camera angle widened so that we could see John's fancy footwork. He was good, actually, but the crazed look in his eyes kind of ruined the effect.

"Oh-my-God," Cathy said in disbelief. "He's dancing on television! The grown man's actually dancing on the news. That's … so pathetic. Your friends are …" She groped for the word. "You moved us back here to be with these bizarros?

We both stared, mesmerized.

. "I could have been famous," Pappas gasped, his dance routine done, "but hey, I had a family business to run. Had to help out my dad. He suffered a stroke when I was eighteen. My chances were ruined."

"His dad never had a stroke—I'll bet he still comes in to the restaurant to manage the place every day!" I spluttered indignantly.

Cathy was starting to breathe heavily through her nose. It was not a good sign, kind of like when a bull is getting ready to use you as target practice. "*You* came back to Hamilton for *this*," Cathy said, her voice raised. "You and your friends are acting like a bunch of attention-seeking children!"

"No, they're not usually like this! It's the damn camera, it makes them act out. I've never seen them act that way, even back in high school. And I didn't come back just to hang out with these guys—I came back to help out my parents. I don't give a shit about being famous."

Cathy stared at me, incredulous. "You're lying to yourself again, Donny. Don't you hear yourself?"

Yes, I am. So what?

The news broadcast had moved to another segment about the war in Afghanistan. I'd sat down to watch television to escape my problems, and they'd fought their way out of the television screen to taunt me. I couldn't remember ever having so many battles to wage at one time.

I hit the remote control. The television died.

Cathy heaved herself, stomach first, out of the sunken old sofa. "I've had enough for today. I'm going to bed. If I wake up in the morning, feel free to shoot me."

"Not if I shoot myself first."

I sighed deeply, and sank back a thousand miles into the sofa, thinking of nothing and everything.

17.

Wednesday, September 17.
10:15 a.m.

I sat in the waiting room at the Saint Albany Medical Clinic on Wentworth Street, across from Limeridge Mall. The walls were painted an institutional green. On one wall hung a print of a painting of generic-looking flowers. I wondered what impulse would possess a person who could actually paint to do a picture of something so uninteresting. A sidetable was host to *Time* magazines dating back to the late nineties. The place was packed. Kids were crying, adults sneezing, some with bags under their eyes, everyone looking sad and depressed, worried, used up, unhappy. *Is that how these people see me?* I wondered. I furtively caught my reflection in the tinted window. *Ouch.*

I was here because Cathy had insisted. After an otherwise dismal breakfast, I had decided to see a doctor and get some help. She was right, she was always right. So there I sat, waiting to see a doctor so he'd refer me to a psychologist to dissect my brain and discover my fatal flaw.

I adjusted my legs under my laptop computer. I'd told myself I'd write the next instalment of my column while waiting. My promise to Cathy to end the columns nagged away at me, ignored but not forgotten. I'd left a message on Bob's voice mail that I had an appointment and would be in later that morning. I didn't have a regular doctor yet—Cathy had us on a few waiting lists in town, but The Hammer was no different than Toronto in that sense: doctors were hard to come by. I knew we were lucky to have the walk-in clinics.

"...So how long have you been lying?" said Dr. Klus, a female doctor in her late thirties. She had a round face with piercing blue eyes, and her feminine hands were in contrast to her strong shoulders.

We'd finished all the medical history preliminaries. I had awkwardly tried to explain my reason for seeking counselling.

I took a deep breath and inhaled. "As far back as I can remember. But not always, just once in awhile. It's not compulsive."

"And why do you lie?"

"I dunno. Mostly I lie to myself."

She nodded understandingly. "We all do that, Mr. Love."

"Yeah, but it makes me do crazy things, like pick up and move, or romanticize the past too much. Then I end up making decisions that are irrational, really. I mean, I know I'm lying to myself, but I can't help it." I heard my own voice say it.

"So you feel that your lying to yourself is causing you to lose control of your life?"

"Yeah, something like that." After my initial squeamishness about unloading my private emotions for an audience, I could feel myself really getting into this." I get scared and my gut's telling me not to do the things I do, but I do them anyway. I'm a liar, and I hate liars, but I lie to myself over and over again and I hate myself for it. Round and round, over and over." I felt the misery dripping from every word.

"I can book you to see someone, but I have to warn you, there's a huge waiting list." She looked regretful.

This was getting nowhere. I had to do something, something desperate. I was going to lose my wife. How else could I get immediate help? I blurted: "I think about killing myself all the time. The other day, I was so depressed I tried to hang myself with a, with a (I cast about desperately for an idea) clothes hanger. I need help or I'm going to cut my freakin' heart out. I can't take it anymore. "*Liar, liar, liar!*

She quickly became quite intense. "Okay, Mr. Love," she said, turning to the chart on her computer, "I'll do everything I can to fast track you. I can also provide you with a list of private practitioners. You could see them within a few days, but they're not cheap."

"Okay, um," I said, edging off the examination table. Suddenly I was feeling panicky. How many more lies was I going to tell? I was frightening myself. "I'll pay for services if I feel any more desperate."

"Mr. Love, let's talk through some of this now. I can't let you leave feeling this way. I am trained to counsel patients who are feeling depressed or anxious."

"I just really have to go now," I said hastily, stepping toward the door.

She hurried in front of me, pulled a brochure from the wall rack, and gave it to me. "Mr. Love, if you feel desperate at any time, don't hesitate to call any of these numbers. There are lots of help lines when you're going through a bad patch. You don't need to hurt yourself."

I felt so guilty about worrying this nice woman. "Is there a Liar's Anonymous listed here?"

She smiled regretfully. "No, sorry. Don't think that one exists yet."

"It bloody well should."

She nodded. "You won't stay and talk to me?"

"Sorry. No. But thanks for everything."

And I was out, hustling past the sickos in the waiting room and then out the front door, realizing I'd tried to take the first step towards dealing with my insidious lying — by lying.

Great. I was definitely on the road to recovery.

18.

While waiting in the doctor's office, I'd dashed off the next Steven McCartney instalment. It was a screeching big falsehood, all of it, but I'd loved writing every last letter of it. It was the easiest, smoothest, fastest column I'd written so far. It had almost made me feel pure inside.

There was a Tim Hortons a few doors down, so I bought myself a care package and returned to the car, scarfing down a chocolate dip donut as I listened to the Beatles singing *Yesterday* on CKOC. Still one of the most heart-breaking songs I've heard or will ever hear in this lifetime. Last night's news footage reeled through my heated brain. Pappas, Valentini, and Reingruber. The Three Stooges. Since I'd left The Hammer I hadn't really found any new long-term friends. Work friends, sure, but none that stuck; I never felt connected to any of them in a deep or meaningful way. Beers after work, or a social barbecue—that was about it. Since leaving Hamilton, I'd worn my past around my neck like a string of worry beads. Had Fate turned me around and sent me back to Hamilton to start over with these old friends? I wasn't so sure I wanted it that way—I still felt pretty disconnected from them.

Cathy was right: what kind of losers started aping for the camera like 12-year-olds starved for attention? Were we all just a bunch of class clowns who felt ripped off that *we* hadn't grown up to be the center of attention? *Was* I really trying to make Steven famous so *I* could be in the limelight?

After seeing them on television I'd felt a mix of revulsion and shock. Revulsion because they all seemed so desperate; shock because I realized I didn't know these old friends, not really, nor had I ever really known them. I wasn't sure if I hated them or loved them.

I stared at my cell phone lying on the dashboard. I wondered if the guys would call me, or if their 60 seconds of fame had gone to their heads and they wouldn't need me anymore. Truth was, any one of us who made it big wouldn't give a rat's ass about the others and would surf that fame wave for as long as he could.

You don't know that for sure, asshole. Maybe you're the only one who'd do that. Maybe you're the only real jerk here.

Tim Hortons was hopping. People left in droves, carrying trays of coffee and donuts. It seemed that wherever I went in life I saw someone who reminded me of someone I'd once known from high school. My brain seemed to be going into meltdown.

I dumped my coffee out the window and screeched out of the parking lot, feeling like some half-baked pilot. My car was practically flying. I felt free and chased and chasing, and wondered what the hell was happening to me. I'd just seen a doctor and was telling her I was suicidal and was waiting for the loony doctor to buzz me up for an appointment. *Oh My God what the hell is happening to you?*

The only thing I knew at that moment was this: I was becoming unhinged, and I was digging it in a dark and wild way.

19.

2:40 p.m.
Los Angeles.

Lou Goldberg was a happy man. This segment on the Canuck hero was a real asskicker. The whole Pam Anderson angle was fabulous—it allowed them to haul out some very juicy photos of Pamalot's humungous cans, which always sold lots of air time. Sponsors loved that stuff. Of course, they were keeping this segment very clean, because, after all, it *was* a family show, but there was no reason that there couldn't be a few sly references to sweaty thank-you sex from Pam to her doggies' rescuer.

And, if there was good viewer response, they could dig up this guy, Clint McCartney or whatever the hell his name was, and get a bit of interview tape. They could use their newest host, Lyra—she had great boobs and would wear anything they told her to. If they gave her the script well enough in advance, she would probably be able to pronounce most of the words.

Yes, after tonight's show, the ratings would be way up.

20.

It *was* a hell of a show.

My dad later remarked that he never realized that Steven had been such a good-looking young lad in his day. The photos that *Hollywood Tonight* had dug up from old yearbooks, Reingruber's scrapbook, and God knows where else had all been touched up a bit.

Steven at 18 had an uncanny resemblance to a young Brad Pitt.

The footage of Pam Anderson's breasts was just revealing enough to escape the censors' judgement, while bringing in a record number of viewers.

The video of Pam cuddling her little doggies up to her gargantuan mammaries was both titillating and touching.

The re-enactment of Steven's selfless act of heroism, as he ran through the blazing inferno of a California brush fire, apparently caught the imagination of the world. Or, at least, that part of the world that got its news from *Hollywood Tonight*.

And the best part was that they mentioned me in the segment.

They made Donny Love famous.

21.

Thursday, September 19.
8:15 a.m.

"And since when are you an "internationally recognized journalist?"" Where did that one come from?" Cathy was steaming mad. After a sleepless and anxiety-filled night, we were both still reeling from the impact of the show.

CTV had apparently sold their footage of my impromptu interview on my parents' lawn. Thanks to cunning editing, I came across like a mega concert promoter: Steve McCartney was a superstar, even though no one had ever heard of him before, his world tour had hit every major city, even though no arena would ever find records of those concerts, and Hamilton, Ontario was about to experience the biggest, most life-changing event in its history.

Even I would have believed it. Those damn editors were that good.

As I sat staring at my soggy Bran Flakes, Cathy's angry drone in the background, something happened inside of me. It occurred to me that I felt calm. My paralyzing weeks of terror had suddenly morphed into a new sensation.

I was going to do something about all this.

22.

Friday, September 20.
10:00 a.m.

I had decided not to call Sharon on the phone. What I had to tell her had to be said face-to-face.

Sharon Munn was now a full-time concert booking agent who worked out of her home in Hamilton's west end. She'd gotten into the business in her mid-twenties when most people from the day were quitting their musical dreams in favour of more stable work. She was the only old friend I knew of in the music business. Although we hadn't kept in touch, my career writing concert reviews had kept me up to date on her progress. She'd become remarkably successful, despite her decision to remain in Canada and in The Hammer, of all places.

Sharon had always struck me as something of a genius—bitter and edgy, but definitely miles ahead of everybody else. To tell the truth, I was nervous about asking for her help. She had never suffered fools lightly, and I had been the victim of one of her vicious tongue-lashings on more than one occasion. Despite that, I had always kind of thought of her as a friend. I wasn't so sure she thought about me that way, if at all.

As I pulled up to the house, I had to laugh. Always the rebel, Sharon had metaphorically given the conservative, monied neighbourhood the middle finger by painting a fluorescent mural of the Ramones on her garage door.

The sound of the door bell triggered massive chaos inside the house. Something that sounded like a small dragon thundered towards the door, bellowing and apparently intending to claw the way through the wood with its talons. I prepared to defend myself with my best Bruce Lee dragon fist.

A massive struggle was being enacted behind the door. Between the muttered invectives and thumping noises, my heart rate was through the roof.

The door was flung open. I was still frozen in my kung fu pose.

"Well, get the fuck in here, Love. I can't hold on to Madonna all day. She weighs 180 pounds, for Chrissake!"

23.

11:30 a.m.

We were sitting in Sharon's sunny little kitchen, eating cinnamon buns and catching up on each other's news. Sort of.

"You're an idiot, Donny."

Still feeling a bit intimidated, I nodded my head. Madonna, a huge brindled Great Dane, was licking my sticky fingers with a tongue the size of my shoe sole.

Sharon resembled a female version of Johnny Rotten from the Sex Pistols. Her frizzy auburn hair was almost in Scottish Afro proportions, and her skin bone-white. She wore blue-tinted glasses. Her clothes were shabby-chic. She looked successful. Sharon eyed me almost kindly. Cleary, she had a soft spot for pitiful fools.

"Fortunately for you, cleaning up after idiots is my specialty. The way I see it, you have two choices: you can hire somebody to impersonate Steven McCartney on world television, or you can go looking for the real Steven." She sighed heavily. "Frankly, if you choose Door Number Two, you're beyond demented."

I nervously twisted my napkin. "Can you find somebody who would pass as Steven?

I mean, there are a lot of people in this town who knew him really well. They'd pick up on a phoney right away."

"Not with the right make-up and lights. Look, Donny, I'm really good at what I do. I'm not trying to brag. I just want you to understand that, if you need people to think they've seen God himself on stage, I can do it." She smiled cynically.

Suddenly, I was feeling a whole lot better.

24.

5:30 p.m.

Suddenly, I was feeling a whole lot worse.

Sharon and I had been hammering out the details later that day over the phone. And it looked like the details were going to bankrupt me.

"The sound and lights booked. Studio musicians hired." She chuckled, a sound that made me oddly uneasy. "Actually, those guys are gonna be interesting."

I felt my stomach churning acid. This was becoming bigger than I'd ever imagined.

"Promotion we talked about—I've already placed an ad in the *Gazette* and I've sent emails to everyone on the media list, but it would be a lot better if we could take out a full page ad in *The Toronto Star* as well." She paused for a moment. "Did you get the figures I emailed you?"

My heart jumped up. "When did you email those?"

"Just a few minutes ago. Don't you have your Blackberry with you?"

"I can't afford a Blackberry." My mind was racing ahead.

"Pffffff. Amateurs."

I was in the kitchen.

Cathy was downstairs. On the computer.

This was not good.

"I'll call you right back," I whispered.

I stood frozen to the spot for a moment, waiting for it. My feet wouldn't move.

There was a strange sound downstairs, like the air being sucked into an atomic explosion a beat before the incineration.

In my own personal horror movie, I found myself creeping down the stairs towards my certain doom. I hoped Cathy didn't have a chainsaw. She was sitting with her back to me. I was afraid to see her face. It was the sound of her voice that was the most terrible. She spoke quietly, in her short sentences.

"What have you done, Donny?"

"Cathy, it looks bad but I haven't done anything yet."

"You were going to take out a 50 thousand dollar loan. We would lose everything. We would be bankrupt. With a newborn baby."

A knifing pain tore through my chest.

"I won't do it, Cathy. I promise—"

Suddenly, Cathy's rage flared. She whirled around to face me, something resembling hatred in her expression. It chilled me to the bone.

"You always promise! And you always let me down! But I won't take it anymore. If you break this promise to me, our marriage is over!"

She pushed past me and thumped up the stairs, sobbing angrily.

I found myself staring at the computer screen.

You can probably guess what I did next.

25.

Saturday, September 21.
8:45 a.m.

I found myself sitting at Tim Hortons, drinking a jumbo coffee. Across from me sat Indy Valentini. He'd taken a break from the Canadian Tire pit stop. His coveralls were greasier than usual.

"Okay," Tony muttered, embarrassed, staring down at his coffee. "Sweet Jesus, it was stupid." He looked up. "That camera took hold of me," he said, clenching and unclenching his fist." I guess," he mumbled, "I guess I just wanted people to think that I'm more than just a mechanic, that I did something special with my life, you know..." He shook his head, avoiding my gaze.

"I completely understand, Tony. I get it. I mean, look who you're talking to—the number one attention seeker in the world."

"Can't argue with that," he said, smirking and raising an eyebrow.

"I'm the one who's the real fuck-up here."

"Aw, you're not as bad as you think, Donny. You've done some really stupid things lately. But you're still a good guy. You love your wife.

You're gonna love your baby, and you're not going to risk it all for this crazy scheme."

Oh my God, I have to tell him.

"Tony, I just spent 50 thousand dollars that I don't have to finance Steven's show at Irondale. Cathy doesn't know, and she can't know, because she's going to leave me once and for all if she finds out."

Tony stared at me, his eyes expressionless. He worked his mouth as if he were chewing a tire tread. I dreaded the words that were going to come out of his mouth.

"You know, man, Angela is no supermodel, and God knows we've had our share of knock-down, drag-out arguments, but there's no fucking way I would ever risk losing her. My marriage and my kids are the center of my existence and they should be yours, too." He sighed heavily, never taking his eyes off me. "I think you need someone to teach you how to grow up. I'm going to help you. We're going to finish what you started. And then you are going to be the best goddam husband and father the world has ever seen. Cause if you don't, I'm gonna kill you."

26.

Monday, September 23.
9:30 a.m.

Even if I had temporarily forgotten about Agents Smith and Smith, they had not forgotten about me. As I was soon to discover, CSIS had enthusiastically pursued its investigations into Steven McCartney, and I continued to be their biggest potential source.

As I was about to back up out of my parking spot at Tim Hortons, the now-familiar black sedan pulled up in front of my car, just like in the movies. The front passenger window rolled down dramatically, and Agent Smith lowered his sunglasses to peer at me like an annoyed schoolmarm.

"Mr. Love, we've been worried that you lost our phone number."

I felt annoyed with myself for my knee-jerk reaction of fear at the sight of the agents, so I was a bit cheeky. "No, no, I haven't."

Agent Smith narrowed his eyes. "Have you forgotten about our arrangement, sir?"

I have to admit that I did feel my stomach lurch at that one. "Well, I don't think that we had an 'arrangement', per se," I said slowly.

"Yes, we did, Mr. Love."

"No, I don't think we did. I mean, it's possible that the, uh, air quality of the room may have affected my memory of our meeting, but I don't believe that I agreed to anything, Agent Smith."

At the sound of his name being uttered aloud in a public place, Agent Smith recoiled back and the window slid up. The next thing I knew, I was sitting in the back of their sedan in the farthest corner of the parking lot, beside a dumpster that stank to high heaven. Agent Smith behind the wheel sat ramrod stiff, facing away from me. I got the distinct impression that he was disgusted with me.

In the passenger seat, Agent Smith was clearly not happy. "You ate our donut," he said carefully. The accusation hung in the air between us.

I stammered back, "But that's not an agreement. That's just a snack, you know, a trans fat-laden treat. That's all." I carefully watched the two agents for any sign of backing down.

Agent Smith, the driver, suddenly lost his composure, twisting angrily to face me. His words were clipped and stinging. "In *this* country, Mr. Love, that is a binding contract. I don't know what they do in *Scotland*, but your parents surely taught you a few things about the *Canadian* honour system. In *this* country, sir, a donut isn't *just* a donut."

As he turned away from me to face the front once more, I thought I heard him mutter something that sounded like "damn immigrants".

His partner took a deep breath and made an effort to speak calmly and evenly. "Mr. Love, we have been very patient with you, but if you do not give us the information about Mr. McCartney that you have been withholding from us, we *will* play hardball."

As scared as I was, the hilarity of this scene hit me. I did something that Cathy had always hated, a kind of nervous reaction to the bad moments of my life: I burst into shrill laughter, right in poor Agent Smith's stern face. The man's expression twisted in confusion for a second, and then the righteous anger of the Canadian Security Intelligence Service kicked in.

He triumphantly held up a piece of paper. "Do you know what this is, sir?"

Gasping for air, I tried to swallow down the hysterical giggles. I peered shakily at the sheet. "It—it looks like an Air Miles statement."

"Do you see the name at the top?" There was a trace of a smirk at the corners of his mouth.

I looked, and suddenly the laughter was gone. "That's me. That's my name."

Now Agent Smith issued the coup de grace. "Do you see the number at the top, Mr. Love?"

It was a zero.

"Y—You guys can't do that! That's illegal." I swallowed. "Isn't it?" Cathy and I had saved up those points for three years. We had planned to get a night in a nice hotel room with those!

Both agents shared a small smile with each other. Clearly, this was the part of the job that made it all worthwhile.

Agent Smith put it simply, so that I, a poor, naive civilian, could really understand.

"Mr. Love," he said, "we can do whatever we want to you. We are here to protect you from yourself. Now," he said briskly, pulling a laptop computer out of nowhere, "which question will you answer first?"

27.

1:00 p.m.

I felt dirty. I felt used. I was a rat, a fink, a narc.

It didn't matter that everything that I'd told them was a gigantic figment of my imagination. Nor did it matter that none of it was going to lead to anything or anyone. Their investigation would continue to yield no fruit.

What mattered was that I, Donny Love, had succumbed. They had found my weakest point, the chink in my armour, my Achilles heel. I felt shaky.

This must be how torture victims feel afterwards, I remember thinking. I know, I know, there's no comparison, of course, but I think that I was in shock or something.

They had agreed to restore my points, along with "a few extra, as a thank you from the Canadian people", but I didn't want to use them now. They were tainted. It would be like Judas going out and spending the 30 pieces of silver. And we all know what Judas decided to do instead.

As the final kicker, when I got home, Cathy was gone. She'd taken only one suitcase, which was hopeful, but the note carefully taped to the kitchen table was not:

Donny:

I guess that you forgot that I know how to check the e-mail. You couldn't resist for even a few hours, could you? Bet you sent that OK to Sharon before I even got to the top of the stairs! (I felt a sick jerk of recognition at that accusation).

I don't want to talk to you for a few days. I'm going to stay in a hotel, so don't call my parents or my friends. No one knows that I've left you, and that's the way that I want it to stay, for now. (That one gave me a faint sense of hope —if she hadn't told anyone, maybe she wasn't sure that it was permanent!)

Time for us both to make some decisions.

Cathy

She hadn't started the letter with "Dear" and she hadn't ended it with "Love". In all the years that I had loved Cathy, she had never left me an angry note. Actually, she had never left me, period. Cathy had been loyal and supportive through every crazy scheme, every risky move. She had voiced her concerns, and those more frequently in recent years, but she had almost always been careful not to hurt my feelings.

So a note with no "Love" in it was brutal.

I didn't cry, and I know that you'll think that I was a real bastard for that, but you have to understand that I didn't really *know* that she was gone. My brain, designed by evolution and/or God to ameliorate suffering as much as possible, understood that Cathy was not feeling love for me, and, for that night, she was not going to be beside me in the bed, warm and familiar and chatty.

So, I didn't cry. Instead, I sat down with a beer in front of the computer and did what I seemed to do best. I fucked up my life and the lives of those around me a little bit more.

28.

Tuesday, September 24.
11:30 a.m.

"You look like crap, Donny. What the hell's wrong?" Tony and I were sitting at what was now starting to feel like our table at Tim Hortons. I wouldn't have made even a mediocre spy; CSIS need only sit and wait for me each day at the coffee shop.

"Hangover. I drank a few last night. I'm drowning in my own lies." I took a shaky breath. "Cathy left me. Last night."

"Shit!" He bolted upright in his chair, flames in his eyes, passion boiling his blood. I remembered the old Tony, the angry Tony, his long black hair jiggling on his shoulders like menacing snakes.

It was starting to rain outside, and a dark grey pall pressed through the windows. I felt an incredible sadness fill me up. There's nothing like seeing someone else react to your bad news to make you realize just how bad it really is.

I sat in a trance for a moment, half-listening to Tony's angry, distressed rant. Then I pulled myself out of it.

"Listen, Tony, we've gotta find Steven. I- I'm thinking that we could hire a private detective. Or we could investigate his...criminal record, or something." My idea sounded pathetic, even to my ears. I wasn't equipped for this stuff— too much *Magnum PI* and other bad TV detective shows during my formative years or something.

Tony, who had suddenly calmed down, looked at me with disgust. "He didn't have a criminal record, you knob."

"Well, maybe he has one by now?"

Tony's mouth curved down in consternation at that one.

Suddenly Reingruber's reedy voice cut in. He was standing beside our table, his big stomach almost blocking my view of Tony. "You should try Directory Assistance. Hey, I didn't get a call that we were going to have a meeting this morning. Does Pappas know? I could give him a call."

Tony was staring at him. "Reingruber, you're a bloody genius."

Norbert looked suspiciously at us, scanning us for signs of sarcasm.

Tony shook his head at me. "What a couple of idiots, Love. How does anyone find anyone these days? 411. Goddam genius."

Reingruber was already on his cell phone to Pappas. Apparently, I couldn't meet one without meeting the other two. It was just like being 11 again. The politics of friendship, I thought cynically.

Tony caught my eye and smiled conspiratorially. "One for all and all for one, man." I felt a pang of shame that I would immediately interpret what was clearly Reingruber's act of friendship as some kind of jealous kid trick. It struck me once again that I didn't want my old friends as much as they seemed to want me. Tony, Reingruber, and Pappas were still buds, and they'd changed together, and they seemed quite willing to add me to their circle. I knew that I was using them. If I hadn't gotten my life into such a mess, I probably wouldn't have given them the time of day. *Real nice, Donny. You'd make a terrific father, wouldn't you? Bet you'd teach your child to be an excellent friend to others.* I was suddenly afraid to meet Tony's eyes, and he knew why, I think. That made me feel worse.

So, to compensate, I went into generalissimo mode. By the time Pappas arrived, we were a well-oiled machine, ready to solve the dilemma at hand. Reingruber had been given the honours, since it had been his idea in the first place. With a face like a six-year-old on Christmas morning, he carefully dialled 411.

"Nothing? What about under a different spelling, like M-a-c-K-? Oh. Are you able to check everywhere, like, in the world? Sorry, this is my first time calling—OK. Thanks anyway."

Peripherally, I could see everyone at the table sag.

Then Brilliant Idea number two came from an unexpected source. Pappas suddenly said, "Wait just a doggone minute. My Auntie Kiki researches our family tree all the time. She's located a bunch of relatives that we never even knew we had! Shit! I gotta ask her how she does that." He was on his cellphone in a flash. Auntie Kiki turned out to be a big talker. We heard far more than we wanted to know about Johnny's dad, the restaurant, his plantar warts, his lack of love life, etc. as he responded to her grilling. But it was all worth it. She was thrilled when she discovered that her nephew wanted to learn the joys of genealogical research.

"Just a little trip to the public library, my friends, and the quest is done," he proudly announced.

We were all elated. In retrospect, we should have known that nothing is ever that simple. Auntie Kiki should have warned us.

29.

2:15 p.m.

Life back at the *Gazette* had become quite bizarre. Bob Chamberlain regularly smacked me on the back as he passed my desk, and he seemed to pass it a lot more frequently now. I had taken to wincing in advance. Meg Cleroux jokingly asked me if I had developed a tic or something.

I had stopped checking e-mail, voice-mail—any mail, really, even at home. There was just too damn much of it. I pretended to be on top of it all when Bob asked, but in reality I was the guy who stops running away from Godzilla and just stands there screaming endlessly, waiting for the big foot to squash me.

So, it came as no surprise, then, that amongst the hundreds of unanswered e-mails was a series of communications from *Hollywood Tonight* producers offering me a chance to comment on the interesting content of several segments that they were planning to air later that week. Hell, it didn't even matter that I didn't respond: they'd always been intending to write what *they* wanted about Steven anyway. Bunch of liars.

I had thrown all caution to the wind by this point. For Saturday's column I wrote about Steven's wild night with Victoria "Posh Spice" Beckham behind the soccer great's back. Apparently, Steven was a great lover, a man of many ancient sexual secrets, the ultimate pleasurer of women. He'd also made love to Catherine Zeta-Jones (before her marriage, because I liked her), Sheryl Crow, and the daughters of a number of international leaders. His trademark exit from these trysts was a fragrant white gardenia left on the sated woman's pillow and a manly nod from the doorway. He was damn good. Maybe better than Clint Eastwood.

Fan response was huge, from all quarters. Men liked his rugged heroism (and the sexual conquests, of course), women loved his rugged heroism and contradictory tender attentions to women, and the teens were on fire to hear his music. Meg announced that a friend of hers had downloaded a pirated recording of a Steven McCartney hit from Europe. We all crowded around her computer to check out the site on the net. I was quite curious to hear what my creation had been up to; I hadn't actually thought about what kind of musical sound he would go for.

The racket that we heard sounded like Boris Yeltsin singing The Sex *Pistols' God Save the Queen*, except that none of us could really make out any words. We disgustedly concluded, quite rightly, that this recording was just a hoax—there was no way that a pop superstar from Hamilton would have a Russian accent.

Where it had taken me many hours to write a column before all of this, now they were pouring out of me like green vomit from *The Exorcist*. I had already written Monday's and Tuesday's columns. They were submitted and ready to go. Bob rubbed his hands with glee.

"This stuff is golden, Love! Monday's bit about stealing intel from the North Koreans is genius time. God, I love the newspaper business." He fairly danced away, humming the theme from the James Bond movies under his breath. If he remembered at all that Steven was "dead" and that all of this was just a big pile of shite, he didn't make mention of it.

On the Saturday night news, I saw a piece about a raid by US Forces on an Al Qaeda hideout in Iraq. They had recovered many sophisticated weapons, along with detailed plans and contact lists for several acts of terror to be carried out against Canadian targets. The General who addressed the media at the White House credited the "invaluable information provided by an undercover Canadian source embedded in Iraq"; well, of course, we all knew that it had to be Steven McCartney. He had saved his country from devastating bombings.

Hollywood Tonight and its competitors all fought to provide the most outrageous Steven news. A major problem was the lack of film footage or recent photos. *Hollywood Tonight* sidestepped the issue by filming re-enactments of important moments using actors. In this way, we were all treated to the sight of Steven McCartney's spectacular pecs and abs as he shirtlessly rescued Pam Anderson's dogs. He looked really good for a guy our age, I must say.

30.

Wednesday, September 25.
9:30 a.m.

The rain battered the windshield as I drove aimlessly around the Hammer. I went past old haunts, down the escarpment to the city core, and then back up, thinking about the gulf that I'd let grow between myself and my old friends, realizing that it had been that same expanding gulf that had made it easy for me to leave The Hammer and chase my dreams of becoming a published writer.

Okay, but I had come back here, and maybe it hadn't been such a bad decision. Hamilton had lots going for it; it was a blue collar city-town, economically a mixed bag, a place where the rich and the poor pounded the same sidewalks and cheered for the Tiger-Cats, where you could go to the mall and bump into your neighbour. I mean, I'd been around—Toronto, Orillia, Bancroft, Halifax, Vancouver, Port Elgin, Los Angeles—I'd never felt at home in any of those places. And my folks were here. Who knew how many more years I had left with them?

I pulled over to the side of the road beside the CIBC bank at the corner of King and James

Street. "These Eyes", a cool Guess Who tune, was on CKOC. I cranked it up, fed off it, the same way I had as a kid in the back of my old man's white Chrysler Newport. I sat for awhile, the realization dawning in me that I had made a good choice, after all, showing my face back in The Hammer. This place had formed me. I got this place. I understood it. I'd never truly understood anyplace else.

The cell phone rang. *Cathy, it had to be Cathy!*

"Cathy," I practically shouted into the phone.

"No, man," he said, wheezing,"it's me, Reingruber. Listen, man. I scored four tickets for the MegaFreak show at Copps Coliseum tonight. It's on me, bud. Fifteenth row, floors. Totally fucking aaaawesummm! Are you in, Love?"

MegaFreak? When we were 13, MegaFreak was it, the ultimate metal band. We screeched our air guitars to "Big Ass Woman" and plastered our bedroom walls with their posters—especially the rather pornographic one of a hot chick wearing only whipped cream and licking her own fingers. What were my parents thinking, letting me put that up? My kid isn't going to get away with any shit—I'm going to raise him like a little monk, I caught myself thinking.

It was ridiculous, a man my age going to a MegaFreak concert. The timing couldn't be worse. And with Cathy gone, I wasn't sure that I was even capable of having a good time. Still, it would be a night out with friends, drinkin' in our old downtown watering hole, and I hadn't had that pleasure in years. It was an offer that I couldn't refuse.

"Yeah, I'm in. I don't know if I'll be very good company, Norb, but I'm in. And the first few rounds of drinks are on me, OK?" I pulled the phone away from my ear a bit until Reingruber's phlegmy cheering subsided. We arranged to meet the others at the Red Ingot at 7:30 p.m.

I was feeling hopeful already. Me and the buds. Just like old times! First, I'd make things right with Cathy, then I'd go partying. I charged the car away from the bank and headed home to get my big ass woman back, before bowing to the gods that were MegaFreak.

31.

5:10 p.m.

I tried Cathy's cell phone but it just kept ringing. I was determined to get a hold of her. We'd talk, I'd tell her how much I loved her, she'd cry and maybe still nurse her anger toward me, but she loved me, too, and there was our child to help mend our pain. I didn't have any specific changes to tell her about; I still owed huge dollars (we owed, more accurately), and my lies were still going full tilt. Actually, as you can see, I hadn't thought about this reunion from Cathy's perspective. I was just running on sheer, deluded hopefulness.

As I waited for a Lean Cuisine dinner to cook in the microwave, I foolishly decided that I could tackle some of my voice mail. Among the more disturbing were messages from:

1. Victoria Beckham's lawyer asking me to call him immediately regarding legal action that his client was prepared to take against Steven McCartney and me,

2. Sheryl Crow's personal assistant Debee, who asked me to call her right away with contact info for Steven, as Ms. Crow would like to renew their acquaintance,

3. the legal counsel for the President of the Republic of Something-or-other, indicating that His Worship would be making a telephone call to my home at exactly 3:00 p.m. our time on Monday to discuss his daughter's recent indiscretion, and

4. four lawyers suggesting I engage their services, as I undoubtedly was facing litigation of a serious and expensive nature.

I listened to a few more, hoping the next message would stamp out the terror I was feeling from listening to the previous messages.

Barry Depaulo had called from the North West Territories. After high school, he'd become an RCMP officer, another guy I'd known who knew what he'd wanted at an early age and had never looked back. He left me his number and asked me to call him. Ted "Wilky" Wilkinson had also called and left a message. Ted had been a buddy of mine throughout high school. He had the head the size of a watermelon, and had played second string fullback for the Irondale Jets. He wasn't the most popular kid, but he also wasn't an outcast. Off the field, Ted was an inbetweener, like me.

I listened to a few more messages then hung up. I was on overload.

All I knew was that my life was crumbling to pieces.

The microwave bell chimed, wakening me from my dark reverie. I removed my dinner, hands shaking a bit, and sat down at the kitchen table. As I peeled back a corner of the plastic to let the steam escape, it burned my hand, making me gasp. Through the window, maple tree branches sent shadows crawling across the lawn towards me, threatening me with more darkness and despair. Soon, the clocks would go back an hour. It would be dark by six. All of the hopefulness that had buoyed me earlier was gone. An increasing sadness permeated me.

I love you Cathy. I'm sorry for everything ... It's all my fault ... I'll make it up to you, I promise.

Even I was sick of my unkept promises.

32.

7:30 p.m.

I waited on the front porch for the cab to arrive. Pappas and I were sharing the cab to pick up the others and then head down to The Ingot. Twilight had cast its magical spell on our street; for some reason I felt that everything was going to work out. I dialed Cathy's cell phone and this time she had switched the voice mail on. I left a brief message telling her that I loved her.

Riding in the cab with Pappas actually uplifted me. I'd had any number of experiences with John back in the day: planted trees down in Flamborough with the Boy Scouts 86th Troupe, saw our first Rush concert at Hamilton Place, played weekend football at the Irondale football field, played road hockey in front of his house, went to each other's birthday parties, got hammered drinking Baby Duck wine over the side of the Hamilton Mountain, played euchre in the high school cafeteria for four years running, and shared a loyalty to the Montreal Canadians Hockey Club. But I'd been a dreamer and had flown the coop so to speak, and John had stayed, content to run the family business in the town he'd grown up in.

"Well, it's good to see you're not above hanging out with us dirty Hamiltonians," John said, beaming.

"It's all good," I said. "Yeah, MegaFreak rules!" I'd made a half-hearted attempt at sounding enthusiastic.

John passed me a flask of rum. I swigged some, and it lit a fire inside me.

I passed the flask back to him. "John, you weren't a MegaFreak metal fan. I thought you were more of an oldies kinda guy."

"Hey, it's a night out, Donny. God knows I need a few. The damn restaurant business." He grimly shook his head.

I relaxed a little at that admission from Pappas. "I can't believe Reingruber. That guy hasn't changed. He's like some kinda unsavoury Peter Pan character."

Pappas laughed. "I know, man. He's a bit of a freak, really. But he's actually got some savvy, you know. Like that comic book collection of his is apparently worth something like twenty thousand dollars, if he ever decides to sell it. He keeps them all in these plastic wrappers. If his mom touches any of them when she's dusting, he takes a hissy fit."

"Yeah, I wanted to ask you what you make of Reingruber living in his mom's basement? Don't you think it's kind of creepy?"

"Listen, I've known the guy for so long that I've gotten used to it. I still enjoy cutting him up, which, I know, is very juvenile, but I can never seem to resist. My theory is that, after his old man left them—remember, he was about 11—she overcompensated by giving Norbie everything he wanted. In a way, she didn't let him grow up, so maybe it's not totally his fault he's doing the Peter Pan thing in the basement. She's still catering to him constantly, but I suspect that he's doing more around the house than he talks about. I'm sure that part of the reason he never left was that he didn't want to leave his mom all alone."

Isn't it strange that I hadn't ever thought about it from that angle? A son sacrificing his right to an independent adulthood for the sake of his jilted mother. Maybe Reingruber was a better son than I was. The thought left me feeling uneasy.

Pappas was still talking. Apparently, Reingruber was a subject to which he had given a lot of thought. "But you know, in his own weird way, Norb's actually pretty happy."

Again, it surprised me that this thought had not occurred to me before now. All of my thoughts seemed to centre around *me*, most of the time. And *that* thought left me feeling uneasy, too. I thought about the look that I'd seen on Pappas' face during the TV interview.

"How about you, John? You happy?"

He didn't look me in the face as he answered. "Yeah, happy enough."

I decided to dig a bit deeper. "Would you have been happier if you'd taken the risks that Steven had?"

He narrowed his eyes. He swigged some more from the flask before answering.

"CHCH. Damn stupid interview." He shook his head a bit. "I really hammed it up in front of that camera, eh? It was like a giant hypnotic eye. And all this crazy shit about McCartney. Man, you know, even as I was saying that stuff about him, it suddenly seemed to me like it really *was* true." His face was suddenly pained-looking, as he turned to me. "Love, you have started some serious mess with this column."

Yeah, no kidding!

He continued, on a real roll. "After the interview, I went home and started pacing my kitchen floor. I kept thinking that maybe I *should* have tried to be a dancer. I mean, I was really, really good at it, Donny."

I nodded, remembering. For many years, as a boy, John Pappas had taken tap lessons at the Lyle Dance Academy. When we first became friends, he tried to keep it a secret, but of course we found out, and you can imagine how much ribbing he had to take about that from his pals for years afterward. I am ashamed to say that, when he went to a couple of local competitions, none of us went to see him compete, and we didn't even congratulate him on his awards. I guess that we were too immature to realize that John wasn't really ashamed of his dancing at all. His wonderful friends were the only ones who had a problem with it.

"You know, when your family runs a business, it's understood that that's your destiny. Your responsibility. I mean, to do anything else would be kinda selfish, right?" He was looking away from me now, out the window. I could feel his conflicted regret. He sounded like he was trying to convince himself, even after all these years.

I was at a loss for words. Too many of my own regrets were roiling around inside my own belly.

He said to the window, "At nineteen you shouldn't be afraid to try anything, man."

I nodded.

With a visible effort, Pappas roused himself back to the present. I could see him choosing to salvage his good mood from earlier. "Hey, at least *you* tried, Donny. And now your column's taking off. And, in a way, you're famous, too."

"Yeah, bullshit fame."

We paused, and swigged more rum. The booze burned the back of my throat.

I took stock of our situation. We were a couple of burned-out 40-year-olds, on our way to a rock concert that we would have trampled our own mothers to see when we were kids, and here we were, sitting in the back of a cab, rolling in the manure of our own self-pitying sob stories. I felt my resolve kick back into place.

"John, this is ridiculous! We are going to get our asses in gear for this concert. Screw our problems, man! We're on our way to

MegaFreak—let's just rock out and forget everything for now. Deal?"

By the time we picked up Reingruber and Valentini at Reingruber's house, we were in a rum-soaked state of hilarity. We cabbed it downtown to the Red Ingot Pub, Reingruber defending the Toronto Maple Leafs against Pappas' Montreal Canadians, with Valentini and I throwing in our two cents whenever we could. One thing about Reingruber that was impressive was his knowledge of hockey stats; he also had the biggest hockey card collection I'd ever seen, all meticulously catalogued in binders he kept in boxes in his mother's basement. He was some kind of collector card wunderkind. *The Hamilton Mountain Monthly*, an east Hamilton community newspaper, had done a few stories on him and had taken a picture of him holding his cards in the basement. He'd kept the clippings and had mounted them on the panelled wall, alongside his baby pictures and rock posters.

The Ingot hadn't changed in twenty years. Situated in the lower east end of downtown Hamilton, it was an everyman's pub—reeked of stale beer and cigarette smoke, and hosted the occasional fiddle band, all of which sounded the same after about 10 Steelers. It was early, so the bar was quiet. Just the old colonial style chandeliers, the dark-panelled walls, the Bud Light neon sign behind the bar, and Steeler beer on tap. We had an hour before the show, so we ordered two pitchers of beer and drank heartily.

33.

Copps Colliseum.
8:45 p.m.

We were feeling the effects of the beer, and we were checking out the crowd to see if we'd recognize any diehard rock'n'roll fans from our days at Irondale. Hamilton is a big city, but it also has a distinctly small-town feel; even in this town of almost half a million, it's not uncommon to bump into an old friend, neighbour, or co-worker.

We bought some more beers from the concession stand and made our way down to the floor seats Reingruber had so graciously purchased for us. The place was packed. The crowd was mostly male, in their early twenties, leather-clad.

The place was jammed to the rafters. Dope smoke filled the air. Walking down the center aisle, Valentini said into my ear, "I'm too old for this shit." He was shaking his head, eyeing the crowd suspiciously. There were a few pockets of people our age, but we felt conspicuously aged.

"Maybe we should have asked for wheelchairs," I joked.

The opening act was called Scream Chamber. They hailed from New York City, and were decked out in bizarre leather masks and bondage gear. Kind of a cross between Hannibal Lecter and the New York Dolls. On either side of the drum kit, walls of Marshall guitar amps were stacked twenty high—in school I'd fantasized about having the same set-up. The lead singer had a voice like a thousand electric razors that made you wince when he sang.

Reingruber was stoked. He double-fisted two extra large cups, spilling beer over the edges, and he'd worn his vintage Led Zeppelin *Houses of the Holy* t-shirt. In the stadium washroom, he'd frizzed out his long brown hair and painted under his eyelids with Alice Cooper style black make-up. It had been years since I'd seen anyone this excited, this frenetic, as if he were still that hopped-up thirteen-year-old I'd once known, hot with puberty and daily injections of Rush, Ted Nugent, Kiss, and Robin Trower. I didn't know whether to cry for this poor bastard or laugh my head off with delight.

We found our fifteenth row seats and Reingruber immediately hopped up onto his seat with an uncanny deftness. He drained both cups, then dropped them to the floor with gusto. Soon he was jabbing his hands into the air high above his head, in the timeless rock'n'roll symbol of devil horns. "Aaaaawesome!!" he shrieked, his cracking voice barely audible above the din. "Aaaawesummm!!!!!"

He started head-banging to Scream Chamber.

41 years old and going strong. March onward, brave rock'n'roll warrior. March on. But you are going to have whiplash in the morning, buddy.

Eventually, though, I couldn't help myself, and found myself cheering lustily. Reingruber's enthusiasm was infectious. Pappas jammed index and middle fingers into either side of his mouth and blasted a great seventies style call-your-kid-home-for-dinner street whistle. Valentini cracked a wry smile, and shook his head at the fiasco he'd found himself talked into. He probably felt like the chaperone.

All at once, and quite unexpectedly, Scream Chamber blasted into a psycho version of the Sex Pistols' *"Liar"*. I couldn't believe it! I loved that song. Chamber sounded pretty good playing it, too. The crowd went ballistic.

The singer, interestingly named Slightly Bigger, whipped off his mask, revealing a face painted with thick, dark make-up. His eyes bugged out just as Johnny Rotten's had when he'd sung the song back in the Seventies.

"Liar, lie lie liar, you liar, lie, lie, lie, tell me why, tell my why, why d'you have to lie..."

We pumped our middle-aged bodies up and down like well-oiled pistons, exactly like the metal freaks surrounding us were doing, as Reingruber's hair whipped through the air like a fuzzy scarf. The beer was going down far too easily.

The next part was terrible.

I'd been so immersed in my head-banging that it took me a moment to realize that a powerful spotlight had encapsulated me in its beam. The band that had kicked its way into the song with a gutteral ferocity now brought that same energy to an end with a screeching halt. Even the crowd of 15,000 people stopped shouting. Only Slightly Bigger continued. But he sang with a softer voice now, a sinister, un-plugged voice. I knew that he was singing directly to me.

You're in suspension, you're a liar...

I was shell-shocked. I wanted to yell back across the restless crowd, but my brain wouldn't budge. I couldn't have come up with words if my very life had depended on it.

Desperately, I searched my friends' faces, but they wouldn't look at me. They silently jumped and shouted to the music. I thrust out my hands in supplication, but Tony seemed to have moved just out of reach. I searched faces of the young metal heads around us. They, too, were ignoring me. I was filled with horror. I wasn't even worth a glance of contempt!

"I'm not a liar!" I cried out. But I knew that no one could hear my thin, whining voice.

Donny Love is a liar, Bigger cooed in that gravelly, evil voice. *Lie! Lie! Lie! Lie! When you gonna stop? You gotta stop,* and now his voice was rising, rising to a terrible, blood-freezing hell-shriek, *or MegaFreak is gonna chew on your bones!*

I suddenly became aware of someone shaking my arm. In a daze, I found myself looking up at Valentini's concerned face. I was on my knees in a puddle of beer at our seats. My mouth felt as dry as cotton.

"Are you OK, Donny? Are you gonna be sick?" Tony pulled me up to my feet. I distantly thought about how strong he must be, to be able to lift my weight like that. The sound of the concert was deafening.

Tony turned to Pappas beside him and yelled out, "I think Donny's sick. I'm gonna take him to the men's room!"

I managed to find my voice. "No," I croaked, "I'm OK to get there on my own. I just need some air."

Tony looked dubious, but I waved him back to his seat. "Enjoy the show. I'm OK, man."

I don't remember how I got to the washroom, exactly, but I do remember the violent vomiting that I did there. I heard more than a few men who came in while I was there comment with alarm.

"Holy shit!" one young guy said. "That guy's puking up a kidney!"

One older man asked me through the door if he could bring the paramedics to take a look at me. I weakly thanked him for his offer but declined.

I sat out the rest of the concert on the cold, dirty floor of the Level 2 bathroom, shaking and disoriented. I knew that what I'd experienced was an hallucination, but I was still terrified, the way you are after waking from a terrible nightmare. *Oh, God, please don't let me crack up. Please just help me to fix this whole disaster. I just want Cathy back, and our baby—I just want to finally straighten myself out. Please.*

I managed to pull myself together enough to meet the guys as they shuffled out in the sea of humanity at the end of the show. Tony and John were craning their heads left and right, trying to spot me in the crowds. When they saw me weakly waving my arm, they pushed through, concern on their faces. Reingruber looked unaware of any drama, a blissed-out, exhausted expression on his painted face.

"Where did you go, Love? Are you OK?" Tony scanned my face. "We were ready to send Security out looking for you."

"Sorry, guys, I couldn't get back to our seats. The crowds were too thick, so I just watched the rest of the show from the top of the aisle," I lied. My voice sounded foreign to me, faraway and thin.

"Can't handle your pop anymore, eh, Donny?" John joked, but he looked sympathetic. "Ah, we're not kids anymore, any of us. This is the last time I drink this much. I don't feel so hot myself. And I think that I just lost most of my hearing!"

On the cab ride home, we were all sunk in our own thoughts. I saw Valentini glance in concern at me a few times, but I didn't have enough energy left to reassure him that I was OK. Because I wasn't.

34.

Thursday, September 26.

Morning.

I may have taken a break from my Steven McCartney insanity, but it had not taken a break from me. I got a call from Sharon at 8:30 a.m..

"What's wrong with you?" she asked in her usual caustic manner. "Hung over or just having a breakdown?"

"Um," I muttered, "I'm fine. Just waking up, you know."

"Hm." She sounded disbelieving. "Listen, I got a few more details screwed down for the show, but it's going to take more cash, and I know that you're already stretched to the limit, so we'd better talk numbers here."

I felt as though I were going to be sick again. I swallowed forcefully, trying to fight down the panic.

"We've got a basic band, but since you haven't got the music selections chosen yet, we should prepare for the possibility that we'll have to pick up a few more musicians closer to the date. You know, if some of the pieces require extra percussion, back-up singers, da-da, da-da. Oh, and I want you over to the rehearsal studio on

Wednesday morning, 10:00 a.m. sharp. Now, here's the good news: I got us our Steven."

For a minute I was confused. She had found Steven? He was going to perform?

"This guy has done a lot of impersonation acts in nightclubs—Atlantic City, Reno. He's got a good voice, and, more importantly, he's the right height, colouring, face shape. A bit of make-up and maybe a prosthetic nose, and we've got Steven McCartney, live at Irondale." She waited for my response. Getting none, she continued. "Look, Donny, I told you that I am very good at what I do, so when I tell you that this guy is going to be Steven McCartney, I'm telling you that even his mother would have a hard time telling them apart." She suddenly swore under her breath. "His mother *is* dead, right? You said that his parents are dead, and there are no siblings?"

"No, no, no relatives that I've been able to find."

I heard her exhale with relief. That made me feel uneasy. "Sharon, what's he gonna cost?" I held my breath.

"Well, I tried to talk him down, but he knows we need him, so it looks like the full price. 10,000." She paused. "Donny? Are you there, or did you just spontaneously combust?"

I realized that, as of that moment, I'd just cranked my debt load up to $80,000 to promote a show that was a complete fraud. A strong urge to urinate hit me. "Sharon, I'll call you back in a minute, OK?" I blurted. I ran to the bathroom and peed, a long and exhausting pee, anxiety flapping wildly in my stomach.

Build it and he will come. But *Field of Dreams* this was not. No wonder Cathy had left me. I was a delusional nutcase. How could I possibly fix this?

And then it hit me. I couldn't go back, so I had to go forward. The only way to fix this was to make it work. Yes, I thought, fighting my fears, we'll put on this concert at Irondale and Steven *will* come and perform. And he'll be great. Just the way he was.

I felt both elated and sick.

Where are you, Steven? I need you, buddy. I need you.

35.

Back in the day, Steven and I had pulled more than a few stunts together. In Grade 7, we'd spent a Boy Scout weekend down at the Watkins Glen Jamboree in upstate New York. We'd called our troop The Turkeys. We were one of 50 Boy Scout troops from upstate New York and southern Ontario, and we'd used our skills to compete in everything from raft-building to knot-tying to lighting fires.

" ... Donny, this'll be smooth as ever. Hear me out on this."

He waved me over behind our tent. We'd just finished eating our breakfast and had headed back to our tents to put on our red sashes for morning prayer. Steven started to laugh as he spoke, that nervous kind of laughter that said we're going to get into some serious shit and, no matter how wrong or stupid it is, we have to go through with it for the sake of making ourselves howl.

"OK, Stevie. Lay it on me."

He looked over my shoulder to check for our Scout Leader, Mr. Jack Redmond. Mr. Redmond had this huge, grunty belly that had hung over his belt, his green Scout shirt half-untucked. He had an eagle eye out for Stevie and

I at all times, as we were the troop's number one shit disturbers, and we'd tormented him on more than one occasion. But he also had a soft spot for us on this weekend, because it turns out that we were winning most of the skills competitions, including the raft-tying race, which we'd finished a full minute ahead of the second place troop. In fact, he was actually proud of us, something we weren't to realize until the end of the weekend, when we were awarded first prize in the Jamboree.

"Wait until everyone sees this!" Steven said, through juvenile bursts of laughter. "They'll be laughing their bags off until Christmas."

Out of his pocket, he pulled out an extra large pair of bright red Jockey underwear. I'd never seen a pair that large in my life.

"Oh my God! Do those belong to Santa Claus?" I said.

"Almost. They're Redmond's, man. And they're going up the flagpole during morning prayers."

"No way!" I said, jerking with laughter. "The Turkeys are in first place. We could get disqualified. The rest of the guys will dummy us if we blow it for them."

"We won't get caught. C'mon."

Stevie darted into the woods and ran along one of the many well-worn paths that led to the Baden Powell Lodge and its flagpole. I started laughing as I ran, that nervous 12-year-old laugh that sprang the nerve between your penis and stomach and tightened it like a piano wire. I knew that what we were about to do was dangerous and wild, but I didn't care. Man, I was 12, on top of the world, and no way was I going to bail on this perfect little crime that would have a thousand kids screaming with laughter.

Ten minutes later, we found ourselves at Baden Powell headquarters, out-of-breath, giggling. We crouched down beside the wooden field fence at the far end of the massive log-cabin lodge. Beneath us, a bed of pine needles. All was quiet. Through the dining room window we could see the heads of Scouts Canada's top dogs as they sat eating pancakes and sausages. The wind furrowed Steven's hair, made the wires on the flagpole tick against it. Atop it, there was a flag with Baden Powell's picture on it, above that the Canadian Flag, and soon, Redmond's underwear. The sun edged over the pines, which had been planted in the shape of a massive horse shoe around the pole and cabin.

"Wait 'll Valentini sees this," he said. "He'll be howlin'."

"What are you doing?" I asked.

Out of his pocket, Steven had pulled a Dairy Milk chocolate bar.

"Cool, where did you get the chocolate?"

"From my sleeping bag, of course."

He opened it, and the chocolate was gooey. He raised his eyebrows at me and I got his intentions. At that age, all of us, except maybe Reingruber, had this awesome telepathy going on. Especially for things gross or rude.

"You're kidding," I said.

A farting laugh escaped Steven's mouth as he squeezed the melted chocolate over the crotch and butt of the underwear. He dumped the remainder inside the underwear.

"I can't believe you're doing this."

"You're gonna remember this for the rest of your life, Donny. And when you do, you're gonna laugh your bag off. Trust me, when you're 65, your bag really will fly off." He checked his watch. "We don't have much time."

He didn't hesitate after that. He scuttled under the fence and the long grass there and ran crouched over to the flagpole.

Steven worked that flagpole the way he'd worked the knots during the knot-tying competition that he'd won for the Turkeys that afternoon. He'd hauled down the existing flags, pulled some twine out of his pocket, and hitched up the chocolaty red underwear. The wind found them and blew them up like a red sail. In all my life, I'd never seen such a large pair of underwear. Once he'd hoisted them as far up as they'd go, he pulled out some thick rope from his other pocket, took one end of the metal wire and used a Chain Hitch knot to tie it to the flagpole. Steven had a knack for tying knots. It would take a lot of untying or a sharp knife to whittle through that knot.

That piano wire inside me vibrated—I knew we were onto something here, and it was going to be big and beautiful and hilarious.

One of the leaders strolled out of the log cabin and started ringing the camp bell, calling everyone to prayer time. Steven hit the dirt and came crawling. He'd dropped his knife. He didn't realize it, and I'd wanted to call out to him but I didn't want us to get caught, so I flattened my chest against the bed of needles, felt them pricking me, and waited for Steven to make it back in the nick of time.

In less than 30 minutes, one thousand Scouts and leaders had converged and surrounded the flagpole.

Steven and I had climbed a tall maple. We sat perched on an overhead branch with a spectacular view of the proceedings—the leaves on the trees had changed, and fallen, mostly. And there was a sweet smell of pine in our scheming noses.

"Attention!" shouted Mr. Miller, also known as Big Bear. He stood at the base of the flagpole, along with the other Scouting heavies: Grey Eagle, Brown Bear, and Hawkeye. These were the veterans of the Scouting world. People not to be messed with.

One thousand young Scouts, with military precision, clamped their legs together, stood iron-pole straight, and shot a saluting hand against their foreheads.

Not far off, I could see the fifteen other kids from our troop, the 86er's, gathered with our fearless leader, Jack Redmond. Valentini was there, and so were Reingruber and Pappas.

The timing couldn't have been any better. Already, kids were pointing towards the sky. I could see Pappas and some others ducking their heads and snatching quick glances at Redmond. Clearly, they had made the connection.

A kid from the troop beneath our tree yelled out: "Whose shorts are those? They're full of bear shit! And they're dripping. Gross, man!"

The heavies' faces fell. Redmond's face went all bloody. He was royally pissed.

A gasp. Followed by shrill juvenile laughter.

Valerie, Reingruber, and Pappas scanned the crowd for us, knowing full well that Steven and I were the perpetrators of this crime.

Steven and I laughed so hard I'm sure our bags did fly off that day. That moment ranked amongst my fondest memories of our youth.

"There they are!" Reingruber shouted, pointing at our tree. He wanted to center us out. We accepted that. That was part of the fun.

Grey Eagle had pulled out his Swiss Army knife, and was pulling the rope alongside the flagpole until he'd reeled in Redmond's' underwear. He set about cutting through Steven's chain hitch knot.

A thousand faces turned and stared at us: two monkeys from Canada, the orchestrators of that morning's glorious prank, perhaps the ultimate prank ever to be witnessed at the Watkins Glen Jamboree.

At that moment, I knew we'd possibly reached the peak of our pre-adolescent shenanigans. Laughing, we swung half-way down the tree and jumped the rest of the way, at least a 12 feet drop. I landed on my heels. A terrible pain shot up my legs but I ignored it as I ran with Steven McCartney into the woods. We laughed so hard we had trouble running down the trail.

"McCartney and Love, get back here right now!" Redmond shouted behind us.

I looked over my shoulder and saw Redmond standing at the edge of the trail, huffing and puffing, pointing his finger at us, and behind him a plug of Scouts cheering us on.

"Go, McCartney, go!" Valentini shouted.

Steven and I kept running. We didn't look back. Steven and I ran the entire length of that path, knowing full well that we weren't going to escape the consequences of our actions. We had pulled a fast one on the powers that be, and, thanks to Steven's scheme, we had our first mass audience recognition. We were famous, man. No drug in the world could give you the power we'd felt that day …

36.

In the middle of reminiscing about those days, the phone rang. My heart flipped. I sat straight as a rod in my kitchen chair. I'd been deep inside the past where touch tone phones didn't exist, never mind cell phones. I bolted to pick up the phone before another unwanted ring jangled my nerves further.

"Hey, it's Valentini. Why are you answering the phone? You should be at work."

"Forget work, Tony. I'm too stressed out."

"Listen, what happened to you last night? Your face was white as a sheet."

How could I admit that I'd lost my mind? It was too humiliating.

"It's OK, Tony. I think that the stress of everything just kinda got to me. You know, Cathy going, and this concert for Steven."

He sounded concerned. "You know, if Angela left me, I don't think that I could even get out of my bed, I'd be that devastated. So, if you ever want to talk about it, about Cathy, I'm here. OK?" I think that we both felt a little embarrassed by our powerful emotions. "Anyway, I'm calling about Steven."

"Yeah?" My heart quickened.

"Are you sitting down, Love?"

"Uh, should I be?"

"Steven's dead, man." He paused." My cousin, Loretta, called me and said she saw Steven's gravestone at the St. James Presbyterian Church down in Jordan. His gravestone's right next to his mom and dad's."

"Damn," I muttered. I didn't want this to be true, for many reasons.

"No bullshit," he said. "Listen, we're coming to pick you up. We're going down to Jordan."

"We?"

Tony snorted. "Look, Reingruber works part-time. Pappas works afternoons, and, anyways, he's the boss. I'm using some lieu time to take the morning off. They owe me a tonne of time. Simple, right? See you in fifteen."

Before I could answer either way, he'd hung up.

37.

1:03 p.m.

We were pretty quiet, the four of us, as Valentini drove us south along Mud Street towards the little town of Jordan. He'd picked us up in his seasonal car—his red '67 Galaxy convertible. It blended right in with the fall colours. Tony only took out this car on special occasions. He'd had it since high school, when he'd spent most of his time outside of school working on it. In his senior year, Tony had won the Technical Department's auto award.

The scenery was as gorgeous as Tony's car. Maple and oak lined the road at intervals. In some fields, there was golden, soft-looking wheat; in others, rows of dried-out corn stalks. The harvest season was in full swing.

The smells of autumn pricked my nostrils. The sun was high in a mostly blue sky. A few puffy clouds edged towards the sun. A turkey vulture drifted on a wind current above a field of pumpkins. Frost blanketed shadows yet untouched by the sun. We were the only car on the road. If not for the fact we were going to visit Steven's gravesite, this would have been a helluva day for a drive.

Tony had turned the radio on low. The music tugged at me, drawing out scattered images of the past. All of us lost in our own thoughts. I felt both numb and intrigued by what lay ahead at the Jordan Cemetery. I wondered how long Steven had been dead, how he'd died, why no one had known he'd died. It was possible that he'd been gone so long from Hamilton that a living relative had seen to it that he'd been buried but hadn't thought to tell any of his old friends. Not everyone put a death notice in *The Hamilton Gazette*.

The cemetery sat next to this country road, north of Jordan. On the other side was Cramleigh's Apple Orchard. The parking lot was jammed. Through the car window, the sweet smell of woodsmoke was strong.

Valentini pulled into the cemetery and followed a dirt road.

"Why Jordan?" Pappas asked, breaking the silence. "Steven wasn't from here."

"His parents must have grown up in this area," Valentini said. "Parents and kids are usually buried together."

"I hate cemeteries," Reingruber said, making a face. "They just wreck that illusion that you're gonna live forever, you know?"

Valentini shook his head, grinning wryly. "Norb, you come out with these genius comments sometimes, man. How come a comic book freak who lives in his mom's basement gets this stuff, eh?" He glanced over at Reingruber.

Norbert's voice was mild. "Hey, you can learn a lot from comic books."

Tony navigated a few more turns and pulled over to the side of the laneway. "I think this is it," he said, turning off the ignition. He motioned his head towards a cluster of gravestones.

"How did you know where to find it?" I asked.

"Loretta told me," he said. "It's not that hard to find, Donny."

We piled out of the car, no longer the four miscreants we once were, but now adults, come to check on our dead friend.

Leaves crunched under our footfalls. Reingruber was snuffling. I saw that his eyes had watered up. He pulled a tissue out of his jean jacket pocket and blew his nose. Everyone else had a funeral face, too.

My heart quickened. *Why hadn't we known about this until now? Had Steven been dead these last twenty years? That would explain a lot. Have I been living in the past for no reason at all? Writing a column for a friend who had never lived to see 21?*

A lump grew in my throat.

"Stephen *McCauley*?" Pappas blurted. "What the frick is that?" He was glaring down at the offending tombstone. The rest of us crowded in.

"McCauley?" Valerie said.

"It's McCartney, isn't it?" asked Reingruber.

I gave Reingruber a dirty look. "Yeah, Reingruber, *McCartney*."

We stood there, dumbfounded, shaking our heads. What the hell had Tony been thinking?

Two other tombstones flanked the tombstone. They belonged to Phyllis and Todd McCauley. They'd died in the late twenties. Stephen, their Stephen, their son by the looks of it, had died in 1986.

Tony looked really angry. "That damn Loretta, she never was too bright. Wait 'till she hears from me. Shit." He turned to me. "Sorry, Donny," Tony said, shaking his head. She's always been blind as a frickin' bat. Plus, she never graduated from high school. I bet she can't read at all."

Out of the corner of my eye, I could see Pappas' shoulders shaking. Reingruber said, "So, that's a good thing, then, right? Steven's not dead?"

Suddenly, Pappas spluttered into full gales of laughter. He was bent double, holding his sides and struggling to keep balance. Reingruber started to laugh, too. He had a high-pitched, girly giggle. It became very difficult to keep a straight face. Even Tony, who was still embarrassed and angry, let out a few snorts.

Pappas had a hard time recovering from his amusement. All the way back home, as we planned out our next steps, he held his left side and groaned, a big grin of pain on his face.

"Hey, Tony, tell your cousin she'd better get some glasses, man." And then he broke out into wails of laughter again.

By the time we got home, Operation Find Steven was ready for its next stage. Reingruber and I were going straight over to the library. We were going to get the Reference Librarian to help us on our Internet search. Tony was going to go back to the old neighbourhood, door to door, to track down any old neighbours who might have had some knowledge of Steven and his family. John was going to speak to his cousin, Constantine, on the Hamilton Police Force about looking for Steven's name on a national databank of criminal records. We were going to find him.

Unless he was in a graveyard somewhere else.

38.

10:30 p.m.

I still hadn't heard from Cathy. I found that I hadn't really slept since she'd left. The bed had lost its refuge status. I watched TV late into the night. You know the score—the really bad infomercial-type late-night stuff. And then the Italian channel puts on its porn-disguised-as-melodrama material. You feel contempt for the whole sorry mess, but, at the same time, you don't turn it off and go to bed. It's crazy, really. All you have to do is to press one little button on the remote, but you don't. When you do finally go to bed, you're horny as hell from all those jiggling bums and breasts. In the morning you feel like a fool.

With Cathy gone, it was just me and my left hand. Well, my right, really. And, as any man will tell you, wanking off might bring you to orgasm, but there's no orgasm like the ones you have with the woman you love.

I vacillated between pretending to myself that Cathy wasn't gone for anything more than a visit at a friend's place, and obsessively visualizing poor Cathy stuck in some shabby sex motel, eating brown beans cooked over a hot plate, or giving birth to our child alone in a small town hospital somewhere, crying with pain, fear, sadness, or dying in the bush somewhere at the hands of a brutal sex killer. That kind of thinking was torturous.

There was no response to my messages on her cell phone. She had done one thing for me, though. She'd recorded a new message before the tone on her voice mail:

I am alive and well. Please leave me a message. Don't be alarmed if I don't return your call. It just means that I don't want to speak to you.

Typical Cathy. Even when she was shutting me out of her life, she still went out of her way to alleviate my worst fears. Loving to the end.

39.

Monday, September 30th.
9:00 a.m.

On the way to the library, my cell phone rang. My heart started to pound. *Cathy?*

"Hello?"

It was Bob Chamberlain. "Love, where are you?"

I had to think fast. "Uh, just working at home today, Bob. Plus, I have to do some research at the library. You know, to keep the Steven columns fresh."

Bob's tone was conciliatory. "Hey now, I wasn't coming down on you about working at home. You're a pro, so where you work is your decision, as long as your columns meet deadline, right? Say, you haven't finished Wednesday's yet, have you?"

"Bob, it's Monday. There's lots of time yet."

"Oh, of course, of course. Just asking. Hey, you're a valuable member of this team, boy-o. Just checking to see that you're doing OK." Bob was working very hard to sound jovial.

Suspicious, I took the bull by the horns. "Bob, are you afraid that I'm cracking up or something? Because I'm not. You'll get your columns, and they'll be great."

Now Bob's tone was almost avuncular. "Well, now that you mention it, I was just a bit concerned about you. You seem...a bit stressed out—understandably, no doubt, but maybe you need to talk to someone about things." Realizing that this was not macho-talk, Bob backpedalled a bit. "Not a shrink, of course. That flaky crap—sheeeeesh. But, uh, a friend or your minister or something. Are you getting enough sleep?"

This kindly advice from Bob was too much. "Bob, please just stay out of my business." I felt pathetic.

"Well, anyway," he said cheerfully, "wait'll you see your next paycheque."

"Why?"

"Your syndication royalties are through the roof! We just sold your column to *The Washington Post*. You'll be paid an extra grand per week, on top of another three grand from the sale to *The New York Times*. How's that, eh? Feeling better?"

A little glimmer of hope sprang to life in my mind. Maybe the monstrous debt that I was in could be handled, after all. And if I could pay off the debt, or at least show her that I was paying it off, maybe Cathy would come home.

"You've got to keep it coming, Donny. This paper hasn't seen this kind of excitement since the Evelyn Dick story." It had been a sordid tale of a wife who was accused of sawing the head and limbs from her husband's dead body and attempting to burn them in her furnace to hide the evidence.

"Bob, I can't write the column forever. It doesn't have much staying power. It's a story about an old high school friend. His story is almost over."

How could I refuse to bullshit some more on my bullshit?

"Well then, bullshit it." "What's Steven up to next?"

"It's a surprise."

"C'mon, spill."

"I've got to go now, Bob," I said. "Back to my research. I'll e-mail Wednesday's stuff to you from home as soon as it's done."

Reluctantly, Bob let me hang up. I hopped in the car to go meet Reingruber at the library. Our local branch had been built in the sixties and had that ugly architecture that had seemed so wonderfully forward-thinking back then. However, it was part of a top-notch library system in Hamilton. We had everything any big city library had, and especially in the computer area.

Reingruber was already there, hovering around the Reference Librarian's desk. He had a shoddy-looking shoulder bag with him, stuffed to the brim with God knows what. Norbert did have a habit of carrying all sorts of odds and sods around with him. When we were 15, we missed the last bus home from downtown one cold February night, and we were dreading the hour-long walk home and the groundings that would inevitably follow. As we groused and trudged, Reingruber pulled a huge harmonica out of his bag and began to serenade us. He wasn't all that good, but we could sort of make out the theme from *Hawaii Five-O*. We could barely walk for laughing. It almost made the whole disaster worthwhile.

There was something odder than usual about Reingruber's behaviour today. As I arrived at the desk, it became clearer. The Reference Librarian today was a red-haired, sweet-faced woman. She was wearing an Aquaman T-shirt, and she and Reingruber were engrossed in what appeared to be a discussion of the drawbacks of having superpowers that only worked in water. I had never seen Reingruber talk to a woman before, unless you counted him placing orders for lunch with waitresses or his mother. I had to practically drag him over to a computer so that we could get started. What finally focussed him was the assistance of our Reference Librarian, Morag.

She knew her stuff. Without giving away everything, we told her that we had to find an old high school friend fast, but that just Googling his name would give us far too many results to sift through. Before long, she had us narrowing our search and expertly checking databases of all kinds. We found seven different people named

Steven McCartney, but none of them looked promising. Still, we wrote down the phone numbers and decided to head back to my house to make the calls.

Reingruber avoided making eye contact with me as we drove home, and I knew why. I had seen Miss Morag conspiratorially hand Norbert a piece of paper before we left, and I knew what it was.

Reingruber had finally gotten a girl's phone number.

40.

Pappas and Valentini checked in with us later that evening. Neither had had much luck, but I admired their persistence.

"You wouldn't believe how many elderly people are still living in those houses on East 19th, guys," Tony said, shaking his head in disbelief. "Remember that old lady who lived between McCartney and the Robinsons?"

"The one who used to spray us with the garden house?" I asked.

"She's still there, and she must be at least 100 by now. I tried to explain to her who we were looking for, but her English isn't any better now than it was then. And there was an older couple across the street who remembered the McCartneys, but they couldn't remember hearing his parents talk about where he had ended up after university."

"What university?" I asked.

"University of British Columbia. Oh, and his parents are definitely both dead. That couple said that they passed within a few years of each other quite a few years ago."

Pappas added his two bits. "Well, guys with the last name McCartney have been very busy committing crimes in Canada; Constantine found

28 who had the first initial S, but none of them looked to be our Stevie."

"Phew! Thank God," Norb added. "I don't want to find out Steven became some kinda rapist or something." This was priceless, coming from our friendly local arsonist.

"Well, we are overlooking a bunch of other possibilities," I said, feeling grim. "Steven could be in another country. He could have changed his name. He could be dead, just not in any graveyard around here."

The others looked like I was feeling. How could we ever hope to find him? He was a ghost, one way or another.

"He could be a spy," Reingruber added hopefully. "Maybe he knows that we're looking for him, and he doesn't want to be found." What could we say to that?

41.

On Tuesday morning, I bit the bullet and headed into the office. It seemed to have been years since I'd been there. I was dreading it.

The reaction from my co-workers was exactly what I had figured it would be.

"Hey, Mr. Hollywood," said Ted Slater from his desk, "what's next, Steven is God?" He was trying to disguise his jealousy with humour. I was in no mood to play nice.

"No, Ted. You're God. You knew that, right?"

Out of the corner of my eye, I could see Meg Cleroux spasm with a suppressed giggle. Apparently, Ted saw it, too, because he scowled and plunked himself back down at his computer.

But it seemed that Ted's question was on everyone's minds, as it felt as though all eyes had turned toward me.

Some of my colleagues were now gathering around me, clutching mugs of coffee. I felt like Jesus, put on the spot by his disciples and expected to deliver a parable, a miracle, or a superstar named Clint Eastwood.

Bob had joined in, as well.

"How's Steven?" Doug Taylor asked. Doug was a tall, obese man, with thinning red hair. He edited news copy for Bob, and was one of the most honourable men I knew.

"Steven? He's good, yeah." I felt like a complete shit. Cleverly and deftly, I steered the conversation away from this painful topic and into more dangerous territory. "Anyone going to the reunion concert on Saturday?"

There was a chorus of affirmation. Meg piped up: "Before Steven's full page ad hit the streets, we called the ticket sales number and bought up twenty tickets. It was a cool ad," Meg said, "but mysterious. No photo of Steven."

"That's what surprises are all about," I said. My throat tightened. Paranoia ate me up. Coming in to get some work done had been a big mistake. It was shocking to me that this group of serious, intelligent journalists was falling for this ridiculous nonsense. I felt queasy at the thought.

"Gotta run," I said, slipping through the ring of curiosity seekers.

And I was out the door, walking down the hallway towards the escalators.

"Wait a minute, Donny! This one came this morning for you. It looked kind of interesting so I kept it out for you." Meg handed me a registered letter, out of breath from running after me.

"Thanks, Meg, it's just too chaotic to write here. I can't focus. Too many phonecalls, the media hanging outside, it's too much."

She nodded. "There's sixteen bags of mail in the warehouse. Do you want to pick them up now or later?"

Ouch. That was sixteen bags of mail that would not be read until Hell froze over. And I figured that I would end up in a good position to know the temperature in Hell. "Uh, later. Sorry, just too busy, you know?"

"I can't wait to see Steven," Meg said. The innocent enthusiasm on her face pained me.

"See you tomorrow," Meg said from the doorway, waving.

I pressed a smile on my face and waved back.

I felt a panic attack coming on. I'd never had one before. That made me panic even more.

42.

9:40 a.m.

I battled my way through the throng of media and Steven groupies outside the *Gazette* offices and squeezed myself into my car in the parking lot. A crowd of at least 50. I could almost handle the media hounding me, but the groupies were another thing altogether. More than a handful wore dark brown t-shirts with the name Steven printed on them in cheap iron-on lettering. My column had created a Steven cult, of sorts. Unbelievable.

I cranked the ignition. As I backed up the car, several of the fanatics pressed against the windows, as if trying to catch a glimpse of their favourite rockstar inside his limousine. But trust me, my old Toyota was no limo. The Clint Eastwood part of the mythology had spawned a fashion trend involving Mexican ponchos and beat-up cowboy hats. A couple of tattooed teen girls who seemed to think that they were at Lolapalooza were chanting, "Steven, Steven, we want Steven ... " But I wasn't a rock star and I wasn't Steven—I didn't even come close to having that kind of talent, on either count.

An image of the zombies in Romero's film, *Night of The Living Dead*, sprang to mind.

I drove the car slowly, afraid that I might run over someone and face criminal charges. The tabloids and TV entertainment shows would milk something like that for weeks. With just enough room, I angled the car down the lane towards the main road. One-by-one, the media and groupies fell to the wayside. A tall, geeky guy with a homemade Steven t-shirt sprinted after me as I sped out onto the road. In the rearview mirror I saw his stick-bug body and his double thumbs-up to me, saluting me.

If I'd seen this in a movie, I would have laughed really hard, but now I only wanted to cry.

43.

10:20 a.m.

Aptly enough, York Cemetery sat on York Boulevard, a main artery that connected Hamilton to Burlington. It was Hamilton's oldest cemetery. I parked the car and went about looking for Steven's dead parents. Even though I knew that this would not lead to finding Steven, my need to know was eating me up. The cemetery was empty except for a few visitors. An earthy smell made me think of worms that I'd dug up as a kid in my parents' backyard, the night before a fishing trip up in Algonquin Park with my dad. The sun had burst through a hole in the clouds and was pouring through the trees, lighting up the remaining leaves on the trees. Sparrows chirped and darted from branch to branch. My footfalls made swooshing sounds through the thick carpet of leaves on the ground.

I thought of the leaf project I'd made as a kid in Grade 3, all those different leaves I'd glued to a large sheet of white Bristol board, the names of each tree printed in pencil under each leaf, the entire board sealed in plastic. It hadn't been very creative—every kid used the same basic format—

but it had earned me three stickers, and I'd been very proud of that.

Instead of feeling depressed by all these dead people surrounding me, I felt a strange shot of vigour. Part of me wanted to experience the dark thrill of finding Steven buried here; the mystery would be over, and then I could start to breathe again. Or, I wanted someone to call me with tangible proof that Steven had died; even better, that he'd just died, the story had just hit the papers, and I could cancel the concert and be off the hook for what would prove to be the most humiliating moment of my life. I waited for a stab of guilt for these heartless thoughts, but it didn't come. It had been two decades since I had seen the guy. What connection did we have, other than a piece of geography and the same momentary pockets of time and space? We had been a couple of baby-faced adults looking goofy in the same high school yearbook. We'd walked the same halls together, but he'd never idolized me the way I'd idolized him. What was I really hoping to find by seeing him again? I wasn't so sure I could handle another rejection, with everything going on in my life.

Wrapped up in these thoughts, I found the tombstones. They sat side by side, under a majestic old white pine. John Allen McCartney, 1930–2004 and Freda Jean McCartney, 1931–2003, each with same words: "Beloved parent of Steven". I felt a deep pang of sorrow. I'd known the McCartneys since kindergarten. Mrs. McCartney used to make

Steve and I grilled cheese sandwiches and tomato soup at lunch. She had a helluva temper, Mrs. McCartney did, and she'd passed that trait down to her son. Once, he couldn't get the lyrics right during one of our famous Friday night, beer-guzzling rehearsals in Kevin Muirsey's basement, and he'd driven his Greb Kodiak work boot through the skin of Muirsey's bass drum. Muirsey had freaked, leaping over his kit at Steven like a wild wrestler. The bassist and I had a wicked time trying to break up the fight.

I shook my head fondly as I remembered that night. *God bless you, Mr. and Mrs. McCartney.* I didn't know what else to think or say, so I just stood there, staring.

At the foot of each tombstone was a floral arrangement. They had withered, but still had some colour. *How many weeks old?* I wondered. *Steven could have brought them here!* I had to make an effort to calm my racing imagination. Relatives, church friends, anyone could have put those flowers there. It was not necessarily a sign from God.

My cell phone rang, making me jump.

"It's me," she said.

"Cathy! Where are you? Are you OK?" My heart started hammering my chest.

"I'm staying at a motel."

"Where? Which one?"

"I can't tell you that right now."

"You're pregnant, you shouldn't be alone. Is the motel decent?" My fears of Cathy cooking on a hot plate in a roach-and-crackhead-infested motel reawakened.

"It's OK, Donny. No bugs or hookers." She knew me so well that I wanted to cry. "Sorry I didn't call sooner. I'm sure you've been worrying."

"Yes," I said in a weak voice. I was suddenly afraid of putting my foot in my mouth, wrecking this chance to convince Cathy to return to our life together.

"Donny, listen. I want to talk to you in person. Can you meet me at Limeridge Mall?"

She wanted to see me! That could be good. Or that could be a very bad sign. "Yeah, sure. I'll be there, honey."

She was silent for a moment. Just long enough for me to realize that "honey" might not have been welcome. "I'll see you there at twelve. At the Greek place in the food court."

"How will I know it's you?" I said, trying to be cute, hoping to jolly her into forgiving me for my screw-ups.

She hung up.

The dead air over the phoneline stumped me. I stared at the wilted flowers at the feet of the gravestones, realizing that my life decisions had forced my wife to flee our home and hole up in a grungy motel somewhere. What kind of man did that to his wife? An abuser? A psychopath? A fucking loser? What final decisions had Cathy made? I checked my watch. 11:20 a.m. I made for my car, my thoughts racing.

44.

11:59 a.m.

Walking down the main corridor of the mall, my heart started to pound. Following me, about 50 yards back, were CSIS agents. Either that, or accountants. *Shit.* These two agents looked more intense, more serious, than my friends, Agents Smith and Smith. Maybe these guys weren't CSIS. That was a very scary thought. *Who else could they be?* I wondered, in a panic. *Who else would be mad at me right now? Who else would consider me some kind of threat?* The answer was: any number of world governments, terrorists, etc. The broad, sweeping strokes of my lies had encompassed everyone on the planet who had weapons and wasn't afraid to use them!

What kind of jail time did people do for treason? *A life sentence, asshole.* You never heard about any Canadians being charged with treason. Maybe that charge didn't even exist anymore. After all, it was a central part of the Canadian identity to slander our leaders and denounce— well, everything. But certain other countries were not so relaxed in their attitudes. What if I were extradited to...Iran, or something? I drew images from all of the most disturbing movies I'd ever seen.

Shuddering, I picked up my pace. Butterflies sprang into my gut and fluttered about. I dodged shoppers and made for The Bay, a store located at the far end of the mall. I saw the food court on my right but ignored it. Not far along I saw a Foot Locker sports store. I ran into a woman and almost bowled her over. I caught her before she fell and steadied her. "I'm so sorry," I said. I'd knocked her purse to the floor, so I picked it up for her. I held it out in front of me, and her eyes grew wide with shock and surprise, and I realized how bad this looked—she must have wondered if I'd intended to snatch her purse. Is that what I looked like to her? A purse snatcher? A small crowd had gathered. "Are you okay?" I asked. She didn't budge. "Please, I'm sorry, I've got to go." I shoved the purse into her chest and she grabbed it. I hurried away, flashing glances over my shoulder. I weaved between the mall pedestrians and eventually hurled myself inside the Foot Locker.

By the time I'd finished shopping, I'd picked up a Hamilton Tiger Cats cap, a green basketball jersey, a pair of pseudo Gucci sunglasses with yellow-tinted lenses, blue Adidas track pants, and a pair of red Converse high tops. There were three guys in line in front of me. I begged the guy in front of me to let me in and he did. But when I asked the next guy, he pretended not to hear me. When I offered him twenty bucks, his hearing was magically restored. The final guy to persuade towered above me by about six inches, and outweighed me by about 90 pounds.

The salesman was busy with a phone call.

"Excuse me, sir, would you mind letting me in? I've gotta meet my ex-wife, and if I'm late, it's over between us."

"Sounds like it's already over."

"What?"

"You said ex-wife."

"I did?" *My God, did I?* Subconciously, had I already written off our marriage? Despair filled me up.

"I meant to say wife. We're still married."

"You go right ahead, married man. I've got two ex's, and I wouldn't wish that on anyone."

"Thank you, sir."

He stepped aside and ushered me in with a wave of a hand the size of a catcher's mitt.

The salesman hung up the phone and rang my purchases through.

A thought had suddenly occurred to me. I turned to the man behind me. "Excuse me, do you play pro football?"

"Played pro ball for the Dallas Cowboys for 12 years."

The other shoe dropped. "You're Tyrone Riley."

He nodded, narrowing his eyes a little.

As I swiped my card on the debit machine and keyed in my pin number, I asked, "Wow, what brings you to Hamilton, Mr.Riley?"

"One of my boys plays for the Tiger-Cats now. Came down to watch him tonight at Ivor Wynne Stadium. Plus, I've got an ex in Toronto I need to see to sort out some legal matters."

The salesman handed me my bag.

I was feeling reckless, so I asked a very nervy question. "Do you mind if I ask you what happened, Tyrone?"

"With my marriage? Or with football?" He gave me a wary glance.

"Your marriage."

He was silent for a moment. His voice was quiet. "I cheated on her—only once. But that was all it took. Do I regret it? Go on and ask me." He leaned into me, tilting his massive face inches from mine.

"Do you regret it?" I whispered.

A small crowd had formed. "It's Tyrone Riley," someone whispered.

"Damn right I do. Now, why don't you get your sorry ass over to the missus and smooth it out before you regret it for the rest of your life. It'll haunt you all the way to the grave, trust me."

"Thanks man." I awkwardly tried to high-five him and ran for the door. I spilled into a clothes rack, knocking clothes onto the floor. I picked them up and threw them onto the top of the rack—I didn't have time to fix them up right.

The crowd and Tyrone were shaking their heads at the pathetic fool stumbling out of the store. I realized how stupid I must look.

I'd just stepped out of the store when I realized I hadn't changed into my clothes. "Damn!"

I fled into a nearby men's washroom.

After I changed, I checked my watch. It was 12:15 p.m.. Late! I was late again! Cathy hated my tardiness; that was another strike against me. Now she would think that I didn't care at all anymore. That I wasn't going to change.

The food court brimmed with pensioners eating their McDonald's Filet-o-Fish sandwhiches and mothers tending to whining, restless children in strollers. As always, a huge line-up snaked out from the Tim Hortons kiosk. The coffee smelled really good. I checked out my reflection again in a shop window. I was a walking fashion crime. *Kids, don't let your parents try this at home. Keep them away from all hip hop clothing.*

But the cool duds were achieving their purpose. The agents were over at the far end of the food court, surveying the crowd in search of one Donny Love. But they wouldn't find that old fool: Eminem was in the house.

Cathy, where are you?

I felt like a moron. Not only had I resorted to lying for a living, I was disguising myself as a some kind of gangsta. What was next? Nancy Grace doing a show about me?

I checked out the Greek place, but Cathy wasn't there. *She got tired of waiting and left. Dammit!* I checked out every nook, cranny, and crevice in the food court, but couldn't find Cathy. Dejected, I made for the main thoroughfare, remembering that whenever Cathy and I had visited the mall, we always parked in the Sears parking lot, so maybe she'd headed down the mall in that direction—I'd run out of ideas and hope.

When someone tapped me on my shoulder, I almost jumped out of my skin.

I'd expected to turn and see badges and weapons. "Cathy! Oh my God, you scared me."

"You're late." Thunderclouds scrunched her forehead.

"I'm sorry, I—"

She lowered her voice to a loud whisper. "Why are you dressed like this? You look like a complete idiot!"

"I know, but don't worry about it. I'll explain later."

"Sure you will. You always do. Let's get a seat," she said, motioning towards the cluster of tables. A coolness had settled into her voice.

"No," I said. "We can't stay here. It's too dangerous."

"Dangerous?" She bored her eyes into me. "Donny Love, what have you done now?"

I squirmed. How could I explain it all. "I'm being hunted."

"Hunted? She gave me a cheerful look. "Donny, *did* you get the counselling we talked about?"

"C'mon, let's get out of the mall before they see you."

"Who?"

"I'll explain later. But if they see you, they'll know it's me, and you'll blow my cover."

Now she looked scared, as well as angry. "What the hell is going on here?" she hissed.

I hooked my arm around hers and redirected her away. She followed, but she slid her arm out of mine.

"I'll explain once we get out of here."

"I can hardly wait," she said through gritted teeth.

45.

1:20 p.m.

"… So then, disguised as Eminem, you left the store to find me."

"That's exactly what happened."

We were sitting in Cathy's car. My neck was sore from craning it over the back seat to see if the new agents were following us and I found with great relief that they weren't. Cathy had wanted us to sit in her car. That made sense to me. She wanted to sit in the driver's seat, to be in control, and after everything I'd put her through, I couldn't blame her. She deserved to have some control over our life. She had trouble wedging herself behind the steering wheel—her stomach was bursting with child. Despite her obvious angst and weight gain, she was still beautiful to me.

Cathy turned to look me in the eye. She was very brave, my Cathy. "Do you know why I left you?"

I swallowed and spoke with difficulty. "Other than the obvious reasons?"

She nodded. She pulled a tissue out of its box and clenched it.

"You can't take the lying anymore. My lateness. The constant moving."

"Getting warmer."

"Well, I don't fool around, if that's what you're thinking. I never have. And I never ever plan to, either."

"That's reassuring, Donny." She wasn't being sarcastic.

A long pause, and oh, how I hated those.

"Okay, the constant moving, the Steven Column, chasing pipe dreams. Never satisfied with anything for very long. Wanting to be something, *somebody*...I don't know. What is it, Cathy? Please tell me."

"I knew you weren't perfect when I married you."

"Okay, fine, I get that. So, what's the reason you left me?"

"*You* haven't married *me* yet." She fought to control herself. "I want you to think about that."

We'd been married 10 years, and I don't think my wife had said anything that heavy in all our time together. Her statement did me in. It washed into me like a mudslide. My heart seemed to have stopped and I was holding my breath. She was right, dammit. Cathy was always right about everything important. I sagged back into the passenger's seat and stared at the dash.

Her voice was faltering with suppressed sobs. "I need you to leave now, Donny." She dabbed the tears in her eyes, but kept her face resolute.

Numbly, I opened the door and slid out of the car.

I bent down to see her face. "Can I call you?"

"Leave, Donny." Her knuckles blanched as she gripped the steering wheel. She'd locked her gaze into a thousand-miler. She'd thrown up a wall inside. Impenetrable.

Speechless with pain, I shut the car door. Cathy started the car and sped out of the parking lot, not a smile, not a wave, nothing to assure me that this was only a small snag in our marital journey. Seeing her leave like that broke my heart. *Cathy, don't leave, Cathy, I love you, please don't leave me...*

I stumbled over to the faceless brick wall and slid down it to the sidewalk. From a distance, people could have mistaken me for some disenfranchised Punker, a surly adolescent, pissed off at the world. Not some messed-up adult writer who'd lied himself into a corner and didn't have the strength of character to pull himself out.

Blackness had inked my heart. *You haven't married me yet.* Cathy's words haunted me. She was right—I'd given her a ring and taken her along on the Donny Love roller coaster ride, the Donny Love one man show starring Donny Love and his faithful, uncomplaining assistant, Cathy Love. She'd finally gotten sick of it. I couldn't blame her.

For years, I'd dragged Cathy from one dream to another. Fragments of conversations echoed inside his head. "Cathy, let's move to Wilno—the houses are dirt cheap there and we can both work part-time jobs and I can write or work on my music without having to work a day job. We'll have plenty of free time. Who needs Toronto, baby?" "Sure, Donny, if that's what you want." "I can't take the hillbillies here! Let's blow this place off. I just got off the phone with the old bassist from Oliver Twist, Jerry Ellison. He's working for Disney and said he'd find us a little apartment in L.A. until we find our feet. He knows tons of people in the biz and I'm sure he'll find one of them to read my screenplay. Jerry's had six of his screenplays optioned, and two have made it to the production table. On options alone, a guy can make a steady income." "Okay, if that's what you want, Donny, but I'm only giving it six months." "I hate this place, these people are a bunch of back-stabbing phonies. Let's move back to Canada. Jerry's an asshole; he's changed from the days in the band. He's totally out for himself. I don't even know the guy anymore." "Where will we go, Donny?" "I've applied for a newspaper job with the Peterborough Examiner. Part-time entertainment writer." "Peterborough ? I don't want to go there, Donny. Can't you find something in Toronto? I really liked Toronto." "We can't afford to move back there. We're too far in debt. But don't worry—this next book I'm working on will be huge. I can feel it! It will even make Stephen King envious. This time it's all the way, baby, you have my word on it." "I guess ..." "My parents are getting old, let's move back to Hamilton. They'll be needing my help soon." "But how will you earn a living?" "I'll drive a cab until I can get on with the paper." "That could take years." "Don't be selfish, Cathy. Your parents will need us, too, one day." "And then what? We'll move to Fergus and find part-time jobs? I don't think you could handle Fergus, Donny. Mostly practical folks in Fergus, no room for wild-eyed dreamers ..."

I considered stuffing my running shoe down my throat and choking myself to death. Or gnawing on my hand until I bled to death. Or perhaps hurling myself in front of a slow-moving car.

I knew what Cathy had meant: I hadn't committed to her, not fully, not with my entire heart. Something had held me back. It felt like fear.

My hands were trembling.

An errant section of newspaper blew up beside me and an image on the page caught my eye.

"Holy shit!" I rolled onto my side like an old rubbie reaching for his upended bottle. I snatched up the paper. Inside the front page of the Entertainment Section was our full page ad for Steven's show at Irondale Collegiate. After all my plotting with Sharon, it hadn't even occurred to me to actually look at the ads we'd planned. Now the enormity of it walloped me. An ad this size was usually for huge touring acts, like Aerosmith or The Who or The Rolling Stones—not Steven McCartney.

Sharon had found a graphic artist who'd done an amazing job; she had more connections in the biz than I realized. The ad was full-colour, and it made me think of the poster I'd once seen for Johnny Depp's film remake of *Willy Wonka and The Chocolate Factory*. The ad showed what might have been Steven, dressed as a wild conjurer, except that his head was bowed forward so that you could only see his black top hat. He wore an electric blue tailcoat and had crossed one leg in front of the other, a sharp pointy black leather toe positioned on a bed of lush grass. He wore white gloves and had folded one hand around the knob of a thin black cane; his other hand faced the sky palm-up; out of it, an array of Monopoly Chance cards floating, as if his palm had produced them. Crisp autumn leaves floated in a ring in the air around him.

From above, a fantastic blue sky radiated light against Steven. Atop the ad, a wild caption written in stylish black lettering: "The Steven McCartney Spectacular Reunion, the Greatest High School Reunion Ever! At the bottom: "Tickets at all Cheapie record stores and Ticketmaster locations".

I was in a state of shock. How the hell had I come to this place in my life? Somehow, an insane desperation had channelled itself through me and dislocated me from reality, making me mastermind this humongous lie. Maybe I was insane, after all. If Steven had seen this ad, or even knew about my intentions, he must surely hate me for it. Maybe he'd sue me, or even charge me with libel. I reminded myself that normal people change; they grow up, they become the people they were meant to become. They don't live in the past, not like this. Most forget about the past; they don't feel an obsessive need to sift through its many layers. And if they do, they soon realize that it's unhealthy, and they find a way to leave the past behind, where it belongs.

I tucked the paper under my arm, stood up with as much dignity as I could muster, and navigated through the parking lot in search of my car. My thoughts pumped ugly stuff around my brain. I slid my cell phone out of my pocket and called 411. I found Tony's brother, Sam, who was a lawyer, and called him. The only way to save the house after the Hollywood lawyers dragged me through the courts, or after the secret agents of Whatsis-stan kidnapped me and put a bullet in my head, would be to put our property in Cathy's name. Even if she filed for divorce, I'd do the right thing and offer her the house. Sam was busy when I called, so I left a message with his secretary.

Despite my powerful feelings of remorse, a strong pressure to escape my problems worked through me and I realized then and there that I needed my writing fix. I was no better than a crack addict craving another blast on the pipe. In the car, I cranked on the Sex Pistols' *Never Mind The Bullocks* in the CD player, and sped out of the mall onto Mohawk Road, shooting down all negative thoughts fighting for power in my mind, focussing only on the juicy lies that would pour out of my fingertips, through the computer keyboard, and find a home on the screen and, tomorrow, in North American newspapers.

But then what? I wondered. Wednesday, Thursday, Friday, then Doomsday. What would I write about then? The no-show? The ensuing riot? Would I be allowed to write in prison? *Give me a blowjob or you don't get your laptop back, writer-boy.*

That thought slowed me down. A little.

46.

3:30 p.m.

No way could I write at my house—turning the corner of my street unveiled a desperate scene. The media swarmed the street and crowded the front of my property. Cigarette smoke was visible above the heads of some of the camera crews. Tim Hortons coffee cups littered the street and lawn. Some faces were recognizable to me—faces from the past, from Irondale days. The fanatics were there, too, wearing their Steven t-shirts. *No way! Not you freaks*!

    I had slowed the car about 50 feet away from them when I realized the fans had spotted me. They started to point excitedly. I ducked the car into a neighbour's driveway, backed it up out onto the road and looked over my shoulder. I saw that they'd fanned out across the road and were running for me, a wall of Steven t-shirts stretching from one sidewalk to the other. They wanted Donny Love, the man who had inside information on their mythological godhead Steven McCartney, who would one day set them free from their pathetic lives in a way that even Jesus couldn't have imagined.

If I didn't write soon, I'd have to kill myself. I considered driving down to the steel factory and hurling myself into a coke oven. I just needed a quiet spot to get my fix. It scared me to the core to see how I was jonesing for this sick, self-destructive lie of mine.

47.

4:10 p.m.

Then I thought of John Pappas. He was a beacon of sanity. I wasn't totally crazy. Not yet, anyway. I headed for his restaurant, a pathetic middle-aged man all messed up behind the wheel of his '92 Toyota Corolla.

A heavy depression settled into me. I experienced a realization that my days of writing the column were coming to an end. Only minutes earlier, Bob Chamberlain had tried to reach me on my cellphone, but I'd turned it off instead of answering it, unable to bring myself to tell Bob the news in case he broke down—Bob Chamberlain loved the column even more than I did.

Sweet Johnny Pappas had found me a seat in the corner of the The Olympia restaurant beside a black gas fireplace. Black cast-iron chandeliers cast dim yellow light that clung to a white-stuccoed ceiling. One wall was painted with a mural of a gorgeous, white, sandy beach and sparkling blue ocean. The restaurant was half-empty. Quiet conversation filled the air. At each table, inside clear glass, sat a lit candle. Behind a shiny metal grill, a chef prepared sizzling lamb souvlaki.

Against my wishes, John brought me dinner and a glass of red wine. I thanked him, and he told me he'd take some time off at eight, after the dinner rush, because he wanted to show me something he thought I'd find quite interesting.

I picked at the food. I didn't have much of an appetite. I did drink the glass of wine. It soothed my nerves a little. I tried to force myself to think logically through my issues. I needed to straighten myself out, in order to; one, get my wife to come back and love me again; two, become a father worthy of my little baby, and; three, come up with a clever way to deflect any of the rage and/or legal actions that would be taken against me after Saturday's fiasco. After some deliberation, I decided that only a visit to a therapist would straighten me out, not that I planned to go.

I watched John attend to the tables. Around seven, the other waiter left for the night and John worked the last three tables by himself. He seemed so calm, so at peace with his work. An easy smile came and went on his face, a big change from the sarcastic grin he wore when hanging with his friends. He was a man here, a professional man running a humble but worthy business, serving up good food for those who needed a break from cooking at home or a change of atmosphere from their workaday, humdrum lives.

John Pappas did what he'd always done since the day I'd run from Hamilton: worked his old man's restaurant. It always amazed me that people like John left high school, stayed at the same job—a simple, average-paying job—and stuck with it until retirement, seemingly content and happy, oblivious to anyone else's ambition. As a young man, I had been appalled that the guy was essentially a fucking servant, yet he was happy. It had seemed to me that everyone should be as restless and hungry as I was. Anyone who wasn't was clearly a zombie.

Now I wasn't so stupid. I had seen enough people who were happy that I got it. Not everyone needed the way that I needed. In fact, now I envied John. I wanted a piece of what he had, that incredible sense of calm and contentment. John hadn't been a slave to a lifetime of ambition and desire like me. He'd lived with a sense that running a humble restaurant was enough. John could have gone to university and done something else with his life, even been a dancer, but he'd chosen not to, and, dammit, he was happy. *Just look at him!* I tried to think back to any job that had made me happy, but I couldn't think of one. *Cathy could think of something. She'd remember better than I do.* I couldn't even think of a job that I'd been comfortable doing. Waitering: no. Writing entertainment pieces: not really. Selling scholarships: no. Delivering pizzas: no. Film business extra: no. Film business coffee-boy: no. Film business writer wanna-be: big no.

The only thing that had turned my crank had been writing the column these past two weeks. For the first time in my life, I'd found a job that I couldn't get enough of. But it was all bogus lies, and it was short-lived, and, even worse, it was destroying my marriage. And without Cathy, I had nothing. I thought of the pending lawsuits, potential alimony payments, the birth of a fatherless child, and coming this Saturday : a high school reunion gala concert built on an epic, outrageous scam.

An hour later, I found myself in John's family room. He lived in a small bungalow on the Hamilton escarpment in a modest neighbourhood. Built in the fifties, the houses were well maintained, with sharp lines and well-manicured lawns. John had never married. He was still looking for the right woman. Tony had told me, in confidence, that he'd come close a year earlier, but the woman had lost interest in him and bailed.

We sat there drinking Coke with ice in tall glass mugs. John had returned with the surprise he'd been promising me since the restaurant. I noticed he had changed out of his slippers into a pair of shiny black shoes. They stuck out from beneath the cuffs of his jeans. His waitering shoes? I wondered, vaguely.

"No offense, Pappas, but I hope you're not going to bore me with a bunch of vacation photos. I'm just not up to that tonight," I said.

"No, Mr. Love, these are *the* photos from *the* day. A rare treat, for only the rarest of individuals. "He sat down beside me on the plastic-covered sofa.

John opened up that photo album reverentially, a buried treasure, Spanish dubloons. The first page blew me away. On the top of the page, hand-written in faded red magic marker: ***Irondale Graduation, 1980.***

Underneath, immortalized behind plastic, pictures from our highschool grad. One of us sitting at the table, Tony with Angela, hoisting a Coke spiked with rum. We looked so young, more like fifteen than eighteen, and yet we'd felt so mature. We wore those hokey, ill-fitting tuxes that looked as though we'd raided our father's closets. I was smiling broadly at the camera—I looked happy. The four of us were there, but Steven's seat was empty. We looked as though we were having fun. The other photos showed us dancing, although it was more air-guitar and goofing off than anything. The last picture showed Tony and Angela necking on the dance floor.

At the bottom of the page was another photo: a snapshot of Steven's leg disappearing through the stage curtains as he'd made his final exit from high school life. From life, maybe.

John saw that I'd been fixating on that one. "I know. Weird, eh? He'd just finished singing *Yesterday*, and I remember the camera had slipped a little in my hands and I'd taken the shot but I wasn't sure if I'd gotten all of him." He shook his head, half-smiling. "As you can see, it turns out I didn't."

I felt some annoyance building. "What I don't get is why the hell he never called any of us."

Pappas grinned. "Come on, what would Steven want with a bunch of leftovers, anyway? Hey, you didn't call after you left, either."

He saw the shame register on my face.

"Lighten up, Donny. That was a joke. Besides, who needs Steven when we have Reingruber? Even after all these years, he's still a joy to bug."

I snorted at that one. "You do still love to bug him, don't you?"

"Ohhhh, yeah." He plunked the photo album on my lap. "Check these ones out. But don't get insulting, or I'll have to hurt you." Then he got a bit more serious."Really, man. I don't want any ribbing, OK?"

I wasn't up for anything that would take that much energy. I began at the page he had turned to. "Oh yeah, your dance competitions."

I slowly turned the pages, revealing pictures of John at Greek weddings, dance festivals, and dance competitions. Several photos had John showing off first prize ribbons. The last picture showed John and his sister clutching a large golden dance trophy. She had on a very sexy red dress. He was wearing a black vest, and a frilly white shirt. Gleaming dance shoes stuck out from beneath the cuffs of a pair of tight black pants.

"That's a big trophy, John."

"Yeah, that's me and Amara winning the Hamilton Dance Conservatory competition back in 1985. It was a big deal, you know, especially for my parents, and it's still a big deal to this day." His voice trailed off a little bit as he gazed back at the photos.

I felt ashamed of our behaviour, my behaviour, all those years ago. Why the hell couldn't we guys just have been more mature about the dance thing? If I had been John back then, I probably would have dumped the lot of us. "This really is impressive, John. I didn't know you were that good." I took a breath. "Uh, I just want to apologize, you know, for being such a dick about your dancing. You know, we were just a bunch of retarded teen boys. We didn't have a clue."

John looked embarrassed, but he was smiling. I think that he knew that I meant it.

"It's OK. It kinda hurt at the time, you know, but, uh, I recovered. Besides, I already knew that you guys were dicks. That's why I fit in with you." He grinned sheepishly. "Ah, let's face it—it was suicide to dance in high school. Everyone would have labelled me a faggot if they knew. I was just so glad that you guys kept my secret. I would have been beaten to a bloody pulp." He laughed. "I figured that, if I didn't give you guys reason to remember that I still danced, you wouldn't squeal."

Memories of the kids walking down halls at Irondale, a sea of Greb work boots and checkered lumber jackets. The macho world of male teens. He was right, the only dancing that was cool then was dancing on someone's head with the heels of your work boots. You could survive dancing disco at the high school dances, as long as you didn't do it alone and were busting out the moves with a hot chick, but even that was pushing it. There were some real bastards who were always looking for a fight at those Irondale dances.

I tried to remember Pappas at those dances. "You went to the school dances, John. Didn't you dance the fast ones?"

"No way. I did the slow dances only. No way could I have danced the way I'd really wanted to."

I felt sad, thinking of that kid who loved to dance but couldn't show it. What a screwed-up world teenagers inhabited!

He folded up the album and dropped it on the coffee table. "C'mon, I want to show you something really cool."

"Okay."

"Can you keep a secret?"

"I guess so." My nerves couldn't handle too much more tonight.

I followed John down into his basement, wondering if Reingruber were hiding down here and they'd planned to tie me up and do something weird to me. At the bottom of the stairs, John turned around to face me. "Are you ready for my deep, dark secret, Donny Love?"

I was growing increasingly jittery. I looked behind me, half-expecting Reingruber to come at me with a knife. Pappas reached around behind a doorway and flicked on a light. "Don't look until I tell you."

"Okay!" he suddenly shouted, as if announcing a MegaFreak show. "Bring your hands together for *Jawwwwww-neeeeee Pappassssss!*"

I stepped into the room, blinking. A blast of music nearly blew my head off. There was a blaze of lights.

Through high-end speakers hanging from the corners of the room blasted that seventies disco gem, "Le Freak". John busted out the moves, big time. Mirrors reflected many Johns as he spiralled, gyrated, pulsated, and twirled to the music. John was coming out of the disco dance closet! I stared at the highly polished dance floor and the spinning glitter ball hanging from the low ceiling. *He has a glitter ball*, I thought, incredulous. *John's got his own regulation size glitter ball in his basement*. I whooped in appreciation, and he was smiling as he danced, like a cloud one moment, down and dirty the next, wrapped inside his own time and space continuum, and I could only think that this was how John Pappas would want to die, in the act of ecstatic dancing and feeling truly alive. I'd never seen him so full of joy. I barely recognized him. He was truly a man transformed.

My sudden pang of jealousy stung me—what an unworthy, selfish emotion. No wonder Cathy seemed to hate me. What kind of person always made everything be about himself? I felt disgust with myself.

John finished with a dramatic spin. As if propelled by a force out of my control, out of my usual comfort zone, I went over and gave him a big, fat hug. He patted my back, laughing, then pulled away and went about turning off his equipment. Now he was just plain John Pappas, Norbert Reingruber's tormentor, snide John, humble and elegant waiter of tables, Tim Hortons socialite.

"That was amazing," I said. "You are some kind of dance god, John Pappas!"

Pappas grinned wildly.

"You should have dance parties, man. Every Saturday night could be dance night at John's. And you could teach me a few of these moves."

"Yeah, you could probably handle it, but can you imagine Tony and Norb discoing? he asked, catching his breath.

He turned off the light, sealing off the dream compartment that he'd built in his basement.

Turns out he had another surprise for me. Upstairs, he handed me a bunch of print-outs. Using Canada 411 on the Internet, he'd found 500 S. McCartneys.

"I've called 50, and none came up as Steven. I've held back about 200 and I'll start those tomorrow, but I thought you might want to try a few yourself. I gave Reingruber a 100. Told him not to sound too weird on the phone."

"Good luck with that," I said.

We chuckled.

"John, I gotta go. Thanks, man, I had fun." I punched him on the shoulder. Then I screwed up my courage to ask him what I had really wanted to know for a very long time. "If you don't mind me asking, how come you never went for the dance career? Why'd you stay here and settle for the restaurant?"

John was quiet for a moment. "I just felt like, oh, I dunno, like the restaurant thing, working with my family and all, was enough. It's a good life. Honest living, right? And I feel like I belong, like I'm pretty good at it. Dancing professionally is a beautiful dream, but that doesn't mean it would be a beautiful reality. Right?"

John's words echoed in my head for a long time before I fell asleep that night.

48.

Wednesday morning I wakened to Sharon's tongue-lashing.

"...And why haven't you returned my calls, huh? How the fuck am I supposed to put this show together if you can't even be bothered to give me a bloody call? You'd better get your ass in gear, Donny, and save the fucking breakdown for later. Got it? Now get your clothes on and get your scrawny ass down here!"

I muttered an apology into the phone and prayed that she would stop. Sharon Munn could tear a strip off a five-star general.

When I arrived at the rehearsal space that Sharon had rented, I felt a burst of hopefulness. The place looked like a real studio, and the air was full of the sound of musicians warming up—guitar riffs and sax squeals, complex drum kit patterns—it was a teenage guitarist's wet dream. This was a professional operation. Sharon had not exaggerated her abilities.

The bassist in the corner was a cool-looking dude, with spiked blonde hair and pink-tinted glasses, easily in his late forties.

"Tommy Childs," said Sharon, who had come up behind me. "Worked a lot with April Wine, Kim Mitchell, Big Sea, and second engineer for David Foster. Very stoned right now, but that won't matter." She discreetly pointed at the guitarist, a thickset man in his fifties.

"Fred Kaufmann. Don't be thrown off by the toupee. The man was Bowie's first pick for every recording session in the last three years. I can't even list all the bands he's recorded for. Just don't look at him. He has a thing about people staring at him." She shuddered. "He gets a little crazy about that. Oh, and don't say anything insulting about Buddhists or the Dalai Lama."

I struggled to take in this bizarre information. I mean, who would have anything insulting to say about Buddhists? Anyways, weren't Buddhists supposed to be pacifists? How did getting "a little crazy" fit in with that?

Nearest to us, on drums, was a man in his late thirties, with the lean, tattooed physique that one often saw in drummers. He had a shaved head and dark sunglasses.

"Josh Craig. Very shy. Used to date only 15-year-olds, but I heard that he had a little trouble with the law, or a parent, or something. Extremely talented." She saw the look I gave her. "Oh, come on, Boy Scout. This is showbiz, babe. A magical world of opportunity for perverts and freaks of all stripes. I mean, how else are these guys supposed to make a living? Delivering prescriptions for the local pharmacy?" She guffawed at her own joke.

She quietly pointed out a sax player, a trumpeter, several back-up singers and a female Latin percussion player who made Shakira look like a nun.

"Last but not least," Sharon said, Stickman. Stickman was an immensely overweight guy, easily six foot nine inches. He dwarfed the keyboards surrounding him. His close-cropped Afro was bleached, and much of his face was hidden by what appeared to be aviator goggles. He was stone-faced, barely looking at the keys, as his huge, thick fingers danced across then with surprising lightness and speed.

When Stickman spoke, he had a Barry White voice. "Okay, my friends, it's now 10:15 and we need to get started. Sharon honey, you got the final program order for us?"

Sharon hustled over to give them the final details. We had eventually settled on a great mix of oldies, classic R & B, and rock classics. Steven had always loved that stuff. As I listened to them play through the program, I was exhilarated. It sounded like we were going to be putting on the best concert anyone could ask for.

There was just one thing missing. It didn't even occur to me until one of the back-up singers, a sexy redhead named Noola, piped up.

"Uh, excuse me, Sharon, but where's our singer? We can't really polish this material without him."

Sharon looked calm and in control. "That's absolutely true, I know, Noola, but he ran into a slowdown at Customs. I've been back and forth with him on the phone. He's on his way. In the meantime, though, why don't you all take a 15-minute break?" She glanced quickly at Tommy and Josh, who were already pulling out a hash pipe and lighter. "But don't leave the building, folks. And let's try to make this a healthy break, OK?" She was already linking her arm in Tommy's, steering him toward a table loaded with cheese trays and fruit.

As she turned to come back to me, I saw the panic in her face. Under her breath, she muttered to me, "If he doesn't show up soon, we're going to lose these guys. They're not idiots. I could pay them twice as much, but if there's no singer, they'll walk. Shit!"

There was a sudden rush of cool air, as the door flew open. In swept one of the oddest-looking people I have ever seen. His dyed black hair was molded into an impossibly high pompadour. A silky red cape blew along gracefully behind him. He wore what appeared to be a pirate costume, and sported impeccable but heavy make-up.

"Dear God, sorry I'm late everyone! It's quite alright now. Maestro Maurice is here!" He glided over to Sharon, holding out his hand. "My darling, darling Sharon," (he said it with a French accent!) "aren't you charming in your little frock today? Give Maurice a kiss, darling, before he begins the magic." He continued to hold out his hand expectantly. Without batting an eyelash, Sharon pecked his huge garnet ring.

"Maurice, I'd like to introduce you to the man who is financing this show, Donny Love."

Maurice uttered a discreet shriek of delight. "My dear, dear Donny, you are a man of vision! I just know that we'll be the bestest of friends. You must tell me everything you can about our lovely Steven McCartney—I want to channel him from every pore on Saturday. We'll discuss this over a nice bottle of Chardonnay and some seafood." He already had his arm linked with mine and was attempting to lead me away towards the door.

Effortlessly, Sharon positioned herself between us and the door. In a sweet but firm voice, she said, "Oh no you don't, boys. We need to give our band the chance to hear Maurice's silky, soulful sounds. They've been waiting for this all morning."

As soon as he heard the praise, Maurice immediately went into gracious diva mode. "But of course, ma cherie! You are absolutely right! I must simply go warm up in my dressing room, and then we can begin. Do you have the items I requested?"

Smile pasted on her face, Sharon was breathing slowly through her nose. I wondered if she had ever practiced transcendental meditation. "Maurice, darling, there is no actual dressing room here, as this is just a rehearsal studio. Remember how we discussed this on Monday night?" When she saw his furrowing brow, she deftly deflected the salvo. "But I know how important this is to you, so I'm determined to make it up to you. I've got champagne waiting on ice, chocolate strawberries, and a quiet place for you to sit and collect your thoughts."

Maurice visibly brightened at the mention of the champagne, but he was not prepared to concede defeat yet. "Sharon, I am an artist. I cannot just haul out my voice like an old handkerchief." He actually sniffed. "I *require* a proper dressing room."

Again, Sharon parried this thrust. "I know, my dearest Maurice, but even when you have not warmed up, your voice is wonderful. I mean, who's going to know? These studio musicians? Please. *I* have faith that your immense skill will carry you through this little bump in the road. Come on, you." Her voice was cajoling, but not too much. *Damn, she is good at this,* I thought in admiration. *I should get her to speak to Cathy for me.*

Summoning great inner reserves of graciousness, Maestro Maurice bowed his head in acquiescence. "Sharon, how can I refuse you? I shall sing." Suddenly, Maurice shifted gears into schoolmarm. He clapped his hands several times. "Alright, people, time to get working! After all, we're not being paid to just sit around eating bonbons! Come along!" Maurice snapped his fingers imperiously at the musicians hovering around the snack table.

Ouch! How can you snap your fingers at Stickman and the gang and live to tell the tale? I wondered. But they didn't even blink at Maurice's behaviour. I guessed that they had seen it all, over the years. Maurice positioned himself at the mike, tying a sparkly gold scarf around it.

Within minutes, the band was into the opening bars of James Brown's "Sex Machine". It was rockin'. I felt like bustin' out a move myself. But Maurice had other ideas. He had turned to the brass section, hands up in the air.

"Please, gentlemen, please! I am hearing far too much trumpet and not nearly enough sax. And am I hearing bongos, perchance?" He glared accusingly at the sexy percussionist, who shook her head. "Mr. Brown would roll over in his grave, bless him, if we were to play God with his music. Again, please!" He strode back to the mike, already taking in his cleansing breath.

He stopped them again, this time more angrily. "There is a humming coming from this amp. Who is our sound technician? You over there? Are you going to fix this? We cannot make music if our equipment is louder than we are!" The gangly young kid nervously crept up to the amp to adjust it.

An hour later, the band had played its way, in spits and spurts, through only three songs. I had not heard a single note out of Maurice. Even the stone-faced Stickman looked as though he wanted to do some harm to the Maestro.

Maurice took on the air of an injured party, patient to the end with the thoughtless people who wounded him. He sat on a speaker and addressed us all. "It is quite clear to me that I have arrived just in the nick of time. I will save this show for you, but you must all help me. Sharon," he said, speaking to her as if she were a distractible six-year-old, "you and I will have to sit down together to discuss this mess and its solutions after rehearsal today. You will need to clear your afternoon schedule." I could feel Sharon tense up beside me, but her face revealed nothing. "As for the rest of us," he said sweetly, turning to the band, "I believe that we need a break. We will all spend some time preparing ourselves for rehearsal tomorrow, 9 a.m. sharp. Right then, off you go!"

As Maurice strode purposefully toward Sharon and I, she muttered to me, "Have we discussed just how much you're going to pay me for this?"

49.

1:00 p.m.

I had turned my cell phone off during the rehearsal. Big mistake.

Bob Chamberlain had left me six messages, each one progressively more panicked than the last. The sixth message contained a slew of profanities and several creative-sounding death threats.

In the alternate universe of the rehearsal studio, I had completely forgotten about Wednesday's column.

There wasn't one.

For the first time in my career, I had missed a final deadline. The *Gazette* had run without my column. In its place was a brief but mysterious explanation from the editor:

Donny Love's column will run again tomorrow. Mr. Love is on assignment today with Steven McCartney.

By the time I had screwed up my courage enough to return Bob's calls and try to save my bacon, I had six beers in me. I felt that I ought to enunciate a little more than usual, just in case.

"Hi there, Bobby. Guess I messed up a bit, eh? Sorry, Bob."

I thought that I heard heavy breathing on the end of the line.

"Bob? Is that you? Cause I'm gonna make it up to you. I really am. Tomorrow's column is gonna be a beaut." I was pleased with my ability to placate Bob.

Bob's voice, when he finally spoke, was cool and smooth as ice. "That's right, Love. You are going to write me a double column for tomorrow's paper. You are going to come in here and write it right here, in front of me, right now. You are not going to leave my sight for food, drink, or the can until you have completed the mother of all columns. You'd better get yourself into Depends diapers, boy, because I'm quite serious here. You just about cost me my job today."

The beer made me a bit slow on the uptake. "Pardon? Sorry, I was listening, Bob, but I just had to...scratch my ear for a minute. Sorry. Say that part again?"

"Love, are you drunk?" Bob was losing his cool.

"No! No way!" I cleverly responded. "I only had six. That's nothing. I could write *War and Peace* on twice that amount. I could write that, Bob. Easily. *War and Peace.*"

I could hear Bob cussing and giving orders in the background. I felt a sudden, slightly numbed pang of concern for the poor guy.

"Bob, man, I know that I gave you a bit of a problem today, but, hey, it's OK. You need to relax a bit, Bob. You could end up having a stroke or something, man. Your health is a gift. You gotta look after it."

There was a strange noise on the other end. At one point, it sounded as though the phone were being swung about by the cord. Suddenly, Meg was on the line.

"Hi, Donny. Meg here. I just need to know where you are right now. I'm sending a cab to pick you up."

I felt like crying, all of a sudden. Sweet Meg cared about me. They all cared about me. They didn't want me to wrap my car around a telephone pole! My heart could hardly bear the wash of love that I felt for my *Gazette* family.

I think that I may have told Meg that I loved her. Several times. And that I loved Bob. Like a father, I think. Apparently, I couldn't handle six beers quite the way I used to. I took a cab to the paper, but I'm not sure if it was the one they called for me. In fact, I don't remember paying the guy, so I sure hope that they had already given him a chit. On the way, I called Cathy's cell phone. I left a sloppy but deeply-felt message of adoration and apology. In retrospect, I couldn't recall hearing Cathy's voice in the recorded message. I wondered if I'd misdialed.

50.

8:00 p.m.

I stumbled out of the *Gazette*. Bob hadn't been kidding about standing over my shoulder until the column was done. Staff discreetly gave me looks of pity, as they left for the day. I felt like the kid staying behind for the mother of all detentions. At 7:00 p.m., my bladder was so full that I was wriggling in my seat, but Bob grimly handed me an empty juice pitcher from the staff lunch room and turned away slightly. He was obviously convinced that he couldn't trust me not to bolt. That was humiliating. I probably should have gotten the Depends.

There was a silver lining to this ordeal. The column was spectacular.

Bob had quietly instructed me as to how we were going to make this mistake work to our advantage. It was brilliant, actually.

51.

The Steven McCartney Story, Part Nine
by Donny Love

For reasons that I cannot explain, I am not able to reveal the location of Steven McCartney. Too many lives hang in the balance. Even my recent visit to see him was a huge risk. Currently, Steven is doing important work in a place that is riddled with danger and war. Guns are everywhere—big, evil guns that are designed to kill many people at a time. Steven's task is to stitch up the gaping wounds of war and conflict in this region. An impossible task, some would say. But Steven has never shirked this responsibility.

I have seen him throw himself in front of a 13-year-old boy being charged by a Jeep full of militia intent on mowing the boy down. The boy's crime? He wrote a daring letter of complaint to the local police chief that corrupt local authorities were draining his and other families of their few pennies of income through extortion.

Steven found a safe hiding spot for that boy, his frail grandmother, and the five younger siblings that he single-handedly supports. Then Steven went to work on those local officials. In the dark of night he boldly sneaked into the offices of those men, retrieving enough evidence of their extortion and other, more terrible crimes to convince even the UN War Crimes Tribunal. He played dirty. He had to. It's a dirty world.

After days and nights of surveillance, he turned the tables on the militia. Using their own ammunition stores, he blew up their base of operation. They lost most of their vehicles and almost all of their big weapons that night. Some of the more superstitious of the militia were convinced that they were under attack by demons, because they could see no one out there in the darkness beyond their blazing camp.

Then he played the most cunning stroke of all. Flyers appeared throughout the community, notifying the local folk that their days of being terrorized were over. He inspired them with a message of empowerment and justice. The flyer was filled with insulting caricatures of the local authorities and their henchmen, many identified by name. The people found themselves laughing at the very men who had cowed them for years.

When the militia arrived in town, thirsty for revenge against their unknown attacker, they found themselves faced with an entire village of opposition. When they made their usual attempts to beat money out of victims, they rapidly found themselves outnumbered. The tables were turning. Power to the people, baby.

This is the sort of work that Steven loves the best. Restoring justice. Ending fear. Rebuilding what has been destroyed.

And he never sticks around to hear "Thank you".

52.

I went to bed that night inspired. I thought of Steven, the invented Steven, that is, and his heroic, selfless missions. I loved that guy. Who wouldn't? If I really wanted to rebuild Cathy's love for me, I couldn't go wrong by trying to be a little bit more like Steven. The imaginary Steven.

I mean, who the hell knew what the real Steven was up to?

53.

Thursday morning dawned clear and sunny, the air fresh and revitalizing. I woke up to a phone call from Cathy.

"Hi. Did I wake you?" Her voice sounded soft and subdued.

I roused myself at the sound of her, my lovely wife. "No, no. I had to get up any way. Are you OK? Is the baby OK?"

"Yeah, we're both fine. Actually, the baby's been moving a lot the past few days. I ... I just wished that you were here to feel it. It's pretty exciting." Suddenly she broke into quiet crying.

My heart was about to burst. Our little baby was a real person, moving around in its little dark sea of life! I wanted to jump into the car and race to Cathy. Put my arms around her and comfort her. Put my hands on her belly and feel our child. Our miracle.

"Cath, why not just tell me where you are? I'll come right over and we'll settle everything. Please, hon. I really want to be there for you and our baby. Please."

She hesitated, which seemed to me to be a very good sign. "Just a minute, Donny." I heard her politely blow her nose away from the phone receiver. She always had good manners. "Well,

I don't know what's going to happen with us, Donny, but I do want to see you. I've missed you so much." And she burst into tears again.

I spent a few more minutes trying to comfort her over the phone. It was an intensely frustrating and disturbing experience, as anyone who has ever tried to do it will attest. When she had gained some calm, she agreed that we could meet for breakfast in 30 minutes at the Golden Griddle Family Restaurant near our home.

I was elated. Things were looking up. I shaved carefully. Truth be told, I had kind of let myself go the past few days. The only clean shirt that I had left to wear was a sky-blue dress shirt. Then I couldn't wear jeans, so, by the time I had finished getting dressed, I looked like I was going to a job interview. It occurred to me that Cathy might be pleased, flattered, that I had gone to this trouble to look good for her. Yes, things were looking up.

I waited anxiously inside the restaurant, scanning the parking lot for any sign of Cathy's ancient little car. This parking lot was poorly designed—a dangerous place—and I hoped that she wouldn't find some old dolt in a massive sedan backing up into her car. I breathed a sigh of relief when I saw her safely pull into a parking spot by the windows.

It was shocking to see Cathy hauling herself out of the car. She was wearing baggy old sweat pants and a faded t-shirt that stretched across her belly. Her stomach had grown by inches since she'd left me. She looked exhausted and pale. I felt a flutter of fear for her health.

Cathy smiled weakly at me as she came in, but I saw a flicker of something in her face when she saw my snazzy clothes.

"Wow, you look great, Donny. Are you going to a meeting or something?"

"No, just to meet with you." When I said that, her eyes quickly filled with tears. She ducked her head down, blindly searching for a tissue in her purse, clearly embarrassed by her emotions.

"Oh, I'm so sorry," she snuffled. "I'm such a waterworks these days. Guess it's the hormones. And everything. I should have dressed up a bit more, I guess. I just, I just didn't have any clean clothes!" And her sobbing went into second gear. She desperately tried to disguise her state from the rest of the restaurant patrons by throwing a menu up in front of her face.

"Hey, same here! I mean, once I was dressed up, I was glad, honey, but initially I was just going to wear regular clothes."

The shaking menu was beginning to settle. "Really? You're not just saying that to make me feel better?" She hiccupped the words a bit.

Under her menu I passed her some napkins from the dispenser. "Really. Hey, it doesn't matter what we're wearing, right? What matters is that I love you, and you love me, and we're going to bring a new little person into this world. And it's going to be great. We're going to be great. Okay?"

I held my breath, waiting for her response. I had taken a big risk throwing all of that at her. What if she calmed down enough to remember that she hated me?

The menu came down, but she didn't meet my eyes. "Well, let's eat something, and then we'll talk. But maybe in the car, because I don't want to cry in front of strangers anymore. It's humiliating. I'm like a bloody tear machine these days." She half-grinned at her own predicament.

For a woman who seemed to be in the throes of an emotional catastrophe, Cathy sure could eat. She packed away the biggest breakfast combo they had and downed two large glasses of OJ. The food seemed to finally calm her down. By the last bite of toast, she was looking me in the eye and even smiling a little.

"Should we split the bill? This is so weird. We've been eating together for years, but I haven't had to think about this stuff—it's kind of like dating again, only in reverse." At that thought, we both sank a bit.

I roused myself. "Honey, like you've always said, 'it ain't over till the fat lady sings!'"

Cathy smiled with half of her mouth. "I guess I'm the fat lady these days."

"You're the beautiful lady these days," I said. And I meant it.

I paid for the meal and we headed out to the cars for the big talk. I felt my hopefulness draining away. I understood what Cathy needed from me, and I desperately wanted to deliver, but what could I honestly say had changed in the past week or two? What could I offer her in these negotiations?

When Cathy suggested that we talk in her car, I agreed, but when I saw her trying to squeeze her big stomach in behind the wheel, I was alarmed.

"Cathy, you can't drive around in this old car anymore. Lookit, your poor stomach can't even fit in there. The baby will be squashed. And Heaven help you in an accident. So you take my car. We'll trade, OK?"

Cathy looked relieved and grateful. "Thanks. Are you sure that you don't mind taking this one to work? It's not as dependable. And it's shabby-looking."

I felt shame. "I'm a selfish idiot, Cathy. You should never have been driving around in this old thing. I should have insisted that you take the newer car, right from the start."

Cathy looked at me with some pity and understanding in her eyes. "It's OK, Donny. Really. I always liked this car. It's got a lot more going for it than most people would realize. I was just glad to have a car." And that was Cathy in a nutshell, I thought. She saw the value in people that others might miss, and she was just happy to have a relationship with someone.

She saw something worth loving in me. She was just happy to have me.

That thought made me feel very blue and very lucky.

54.

I would like to be able to say that Cathy and I had a great talk, that we worked out the problems plaguing our relationship, that we were finally reunited with a long, passionate kiss, sitting in that car, but I can't.

We didn't get to the conversation or the kiss.

As I was gazing in pained love at my estranged wife, two black sedans pulled up rapidly behind and in front of the car, cutting off our way out of the lot. My initial response was to gear up to blast Agents Smith and Smith for this intrusion. I knew that they had been tapping my phone and keeping me constantly under surveillance, but they were usually polite enough to stay back, settling for the occasional sheepish wave when I forced them into it. But this, this was unacceptable! And at *this* moment, of all times!

As I opened my mouth to protest loudly, it hit me that the black-suited figures emerging rapidly from the cars were not my CSIS agents. Before I could say a word, strong hands were hauling me out of the car. I felt a jab in my thigh. I looked over at Cathy in anguish, as she was being pried out of the passenger side. Cathy had the good sense to fight back. She wasn't normally that strong, but some desperate mother-to-be instincts seemed to have kicked in, and she was definitely giving them a hard time. I started a roar of rage at their treatment of her, but felt myself become strangely numb and sleepy. I felt myself being tossed into the back seat of one of the sedans. As I began to lose consciousness, I felt a muffled surge of hope as I looked out the sedan's tinted window.

As we pulled away, I saw that a third black sedan had pulled up behind the second. It was Agents Smith and Smith. And they definitely weren't letting these mystery men take Cathy. Agent Smith had forcefully stepped in between the kidnappers and Cathy.

My heroes.

55.

You know how, in all the spy movies, when an agent is kidnapped by the enemy, he comes to in a bare, windowless cell, with a bulb hanging down? I came to in a four-star hotel room.

Seriously. There were chocolates on the pillows.

The mystery men had apparently administered something to waken me. There were several of them leaning down over me. I felt bleary and cotton-mouthed.

An older man with bad breath spoke first. His voice had the ring of authority.

"Mr. Love, I am an agent of the government of the United States of America. You are in our custody to answer some questions regarding homeland security and the welfare of the United States and its citizens. You will be released, unharmed, when you have satisfactorily shared the information that we require. If, however, you are uncooperative, or we have reason to believe that you are a continuing threat, we will detain you indefinitely. We have the authority to do so, so we do not make this threat lightly. Do you understand what I am saying to you, sir? Mr. Love?" He was frowning down at me. I had the feeling that I ought to be very afraid, but I still felt a bit odd from the drugs they had given me.

I tried to gather up my senses. I would intimidate them with my journalistic knowledge of my own rights. This is what I was trying to say: "You have no right to hold me. Are you arresting me? Where is the warrant? And I want a phonecall right now." That is not what came out.

They all looked quite perplexed at my slurry mumblings. A younger man angrily hissed at another, "Shit, Frank, you gave him too much stuff! He can't even talk, for Chrissake!"

As the man prepared to retort, the older man in charge stifled him with a glance. He drew himself up taller, overcoming the embarrassment of this little miscalulation. "Mr. Love," he spoke quite slowly and clearly for my benefit," it appears that you are feeling quite sleepy right now, but we need you to be alert for our interview, so we will be giving you a little something to help you to wake up, alright?"

When that injection kicked in, I felt myself improve rapidly. In fact, I felt really good. Really.

"Mr. Love, we are recording this interview. Please answer the questions directly, thoroughly, and honestly. As I have informed you already, your failure to do so will ensure that you will be in our custody for an indefinite period of time. Now," the older man began, glancing at a laptop screen, "when did you last see Steven McCartney?"

I felt fear leaping about inside my stomach. The last time that I had answered honestly, it had gotten me nowhere. *What should I say?!*

I decided to tell them to screw off. I mean, what could they do to me, really? I was a Canadian citizen. They had no jurisdiction over me. Hey, they had drugged and abducted me! That wasn't legal, except in the movies. And this was no spy movie. Clearly. Good God, there were imitation Louis XIV armchairs in this hotel prison room!

As I opened my mouth, my brain moved with alarming speed to images of other men who were not Americans, either. Men who, even now, were wasting away in Guantanamo Bay, or in mobile CIA torture units flying over undisclosed European countries. Men whose countries governments could not, or would not, do anything to rescue them. I shut my mouth rapidly. I had a child. A wife. I had to be sensible about this.

The young man who had lost his temper about my drug dosage was now staring at my legs. In curiosity, I glanced down, too. My legs were jumping up and down like loosed firehoses. My fingers also had a mind of their own. They were twisted up in a kind of sign language for the insane.

"What the hell's wrong with me?" I croaked, frightened. My voice was cracking. "Make'em stop!"

Cursing under his breath, the young man was running toward a black case on the table. He grabbed a needle and a small bottle and came running back. Meanwhile, two other agents had grabbed my wildly flailing limbs and were forcing them down until the shot could be administered. I felt a strange, crazy laugh erupt up out of my throat involuntarily

"Heeeee-heee-heeeeeeee-heeeee," I wheezed. The wildest laughter flew out of me in endless spirals. I saw one of the men twitch at the mouth, then catch himself in alarm. Just the sound of my own shrieking made me want to laugh, the way that kids get each other going at a party. "Hawrrr—HHHawreeeeee!———" I guffawed.

"Give him the shot fast, before we all lose it, Davis!" one of the men muttered, between strange hiccupping breaths. He kept his face turned away from me as he ground down on my jimmy legs.

"No names!" the older man reminded him, angrily.

The younger man bent towards me, preparing to insert the needle into the bottle. At that precise moment, the man holding my legs lost his grip, and my left leg flew upward spasmodically, knocking the bottle from the agent's hand. It shattered against the far wall. The agents stared at me, mouths open.

Thrusting my legs back down, one agent struggled to keep a high-pitched giggle down. My own laughter showed no signs of slowing.

"Agent!" the older man said in a warning tone.

"Sorry, sir," was the muffled reply.

"Please make it stop!" I gasped. "It's killing my stomach. Owwww—eeeheeeeheeeee!"

Over the din, I heard the older man's cell phone ring. He stepped back into the bathroom to speak into it. When he came out, his face was black with barely controlled fury.

"Agents, our interview with Mr. Love is over. We are to hand him over to CSIS immediately."

He held up his hands against the volley of frustrated shouts. "I know, men, I know, but I don't make these decisions."

"Where do we have to take him?" asked the young agent. He had to raise his voice to be heard above the sound of my shrieking.

The older man looked sour. "They've apparently been waiting outside this door for the last twenty minutes."

They had a bit of a time getting me over to the door. I couldn't really walk on my jimmy legs, and they couldn't really carry me because I was spasming about so much. In the end, I was dragged to the door in a rather undignified manner. I would have been embarrassed if I hadn't been too busy laughing like a psycho.

Agents Smith and several colleagues looked very grim indeed when the door opened. In fact, there were thunderclouds all round. I guess that, in the game of high stakes intelligence, nobody likes to look like they've lost.

"Would you be so kind as to tell us what you have poisoned him with, so that we can help him?" said Agent Smith through gritted teeth.

"That's classified information," smirked the leader of the Americans. "We'll get him next time."

Agent Smith had already turned heel to follow the men who were struggling to drag me down the hall. He looked really furious. I tried not to laugh too loudly as we careered down the hall and into the elevator, but at least one hotel visitor got an earful.

I caught an alarming glimpse of my wild, flailing self in the smoky mirrors of the beautifully appointed hotel elevator.

It really was a very elegant hotel.

56.

Thursday night.
11:00 p.m.

I wasn't spazzing out anymore. Agent Smith had carefully researched the drug choices of my US kidnappers, and had decided on a safe middle-of-the-road antidote: Tylenol. That was the Canadian way.

"We don't want to pump more chemicals into your body, Mr. Love. That stuff will kill you. The human body can take only so much abuse. That's the problem with those guys from south of the border. Really indiscriminate about these things." Agents Smith and Smith were enjoying large double doubles and a box of Tim Hortons donuts. They seemed to be unaware of the irony of their observations.

Right off the bat, they had reassured me that Cathy was fine. "We absolutely would not have permitted Mrs. Love to be taken by the interloping agents," Agent Smith declared. "Mrs. Love is aware that you are safely home. She is resting at the Royal Connaught tonight, in the penthouse suite with full room service, courtesy of the Canadian taxpayer. It was the least that we could do for her. Nice lady."

"Pregnant woman in that rat hole hotel that she was in—shameful," muttered the other agent.

I felt like a real asshole.

I was sitting at my kitchen table, desperately trying to start the final column about Steven. Deadline was 1:00 am, and that was with an extension from Bob, who had had a private visit from my CSIS agents and couldn't very well say no.

Agent Smith eyed me over the rim of his cup. "It's getting late, Mr. Love. We have an agreement. Just because we're not drugging you to get some answers doesn't mean that we aren't in an official interview here."

I nervously played with the salt shaker. "I know, I promise. I just really need to get this column in, guys. It's the last one, and everything rides on this baby." I thought of Cathy, of how close we were to reconciling, and I had a strong sense of impending change. This felt like an important moment, and I really didn't want to mess it up. I listened to the quiet chatting of the two agents in my kitchen as they fixed themselves a snack. For two experts in intelligence-gathering, they sure had a hard time deciding on what kind of mustard to put on their ham sandwiches. I felt a sudden sense of calm. It was a very nice feeling, and one that I hadn't had in a very long time.

I knew what I wanted to write. The words flowed out of me naturally—not in a sick, vomiting way, as they had for so many of my earlier Steven columns. I finished it fast. The agents were still eating when I closed the lid on the laptop and sat back.

I sat quietly for a few minutes, enjoying the domestic peace of the scene. When Agents Smith finally finished their snack, we all got down to business.

Agent Smith stared down at the table top for a moment before he began. His mouth was set.

"Mr. Love, you opened a huge can of worms with these columns. I can't tell you how many man hours our agency has spent on this investigation. We have followed every lead, in many different countries, and, as you saw today, we had to ruffle a few feathers along the road, which is not the Canadian way. After all of this work, we have been instructed to drop the case, because of budgetary restrictions."

The other Agent Smith humphed discreetly in frustration.

Agent Smith continued. "Our superiors believe that there simply isn't enough threat to this case to justify the expense. Apparently, there is a new top priority at the Agency; something to do with contaminated food imports from China, but you didn't hear that from me." Another humph of disgust from Agent Smith. "However, before we close this investigation, my partner and I have several questions that we expect you to answer honestly." He levelled his gaze at me. "Number one: Is Steven McCartney alive?"

I guessed that I could give the truth another try. "I don't know. I haven't seen him, heard from him, or even heard *of* him in over 20 years." I waited nervously for the reaction.

Agent Smith stared at me intensely. He worked his mouth a little. "Number two: Where did you get the information for your stories about Mr. McCartney?"

"Look, guys, I'm sorry to have to say this, but I tried to tell you the truth at the beginning and you wouldn't believe me. I made it all up. Every last crazy bit of it. Totally imaginary. C'mon—Clint Eastwood? Even Clint Eastwood isn't really Clint Eastwood, if you know what I mean." Agent Smith was nodding his head, brow furrowed, but Agent Smith looked pissed off.

"Do we look like men who have time for shenanigans, Mr. Love? Because we don't. Not at all. We have important work to do to protect this great nation from all kinds of threats, so we don't have time for Grade 8 hijinks." He scowled and turned his head away in disgust.

I felt ashamed of myself. I really had wasted their time. And all to chase something that people who've grown up know is not worth chasing.

As they headed out the door, I ran to hold it open. "I wanted Steven to be real. My version of Steven, you know?"

Agent Smith turned back to me and grinned. "Yah, he would have been a helluva man, Mr. Love. A real hero." The other agent looked sour behind the wheel as they backed down the driveway.

57.

Friday October 4, 2007.
11:00 p.m.

As I walked into Tim Hortons, Cathy's voice echoed inside my head from our phone conversation that morning. *"Donny, we need to have that talk now. I'll see you at the house at noon."*

Carrying my coffee past Tony, I noticed he'd circled a want-ad looking for a mechanic at Cayuga Speedway. *Very interesting, Tony, Mr. Who-Needs-A-Dream.* I pretended I didn't notice and took my spot at our table. Pappas and Reingruber sat in their respective seats.

The place was packed with old people. Outside, the sun fought to break through the cloud cover. Beyond the usual salutations, no one was very talkative.

I could tell by their mood that everyone had read my final column.

After an awkward silence, Reingruber said, "I'm kind of sad this has to end."

"That what has to end?" said Tony. "Say what you mean, goddamit."

"Well, you know, the search."

"Yeah," I said. "Me, too."

"It gave us something to hope for, I think," John said. "For a while there, I felt Steven was our friend again. Like we were going to find him and he'd come back and ... we'd start over. That would have been nice."

"Yeah, like maybe he'd move back here like you did, Donny," said Reingruber. "That would have been cool."

"Thanks," I said, staring into my coffee.

"Well, I'm glad this bullshit search is over," Tony said. "It was totally nuts."

"Of course it was totally nuts," said John. "But, if you think about it, it was probably the most fun we've had since high school."

"The most fun since high school, eh, John?" Tony was glaring at John. "Well then, your life really has been pathetic."

"You're disappointed, too, Tony. Admit it," John said.

Tony went back to his paper and said nothing. It occurred to me that he was hurting.

"I thought this whole Making Steven Famous thing was magical," said Reingruber. "For a moment, it seemed as though he was really going to come back, just like Jesus, man."

"Magical?" I said. "I never thought of it that way, but, in a way, I can see it. It was kind of magical. Hey Tony," I said, trying to break his tough facade, "why don't you tell us what you circled in the newspaper?"

"None of your business," he said, rising with paper in hand. He tucked it under the arm of his coveralls. "Break's over. Back to work."

"I gotta go, too," Reingruber piped up.

"Since when do you have to go anywhere?" John said.

"I have a date."

"A date?" John laughed in disbelief. "With who, your mother?"

Reingruber remained unflappable. "Very funny, Pappas. Actually, Morag and I are checking out a storefront lease today. She thinks I'd be really good at running my own collector card shop."

We stared after Reingruber, open-mouthed. He gave us a wave as he headed off on his 10-speed bike.

John looked perplexed. "Morag? Who's Morag?"

I had to laugh at his expression. "The librarian. Remember I told you about that?"

John was still trying to fathom this new facet of Reingruber.

"Hey, Donny," Tony said, turning to face me outside. "Maybe Steven didn't come back to The Hammer, but you did ... and I'm glad you did." He smiled at me, turned and headed for the Canadian Tire.

That was the closest I'd ever seen Tony to telling me he cared about me.

"So, now what, John?" I asked.

He grinned at me sideways. "Dance lessons."

"Dance lessons?" I said. "Are you serious?"

"Yep. I've been stuck in a rut. I need to work on a new style."

"Good for you, man."

"See you at the show tomorrow," he said, stepping off the curb.

I checked my watch. 11:30 a.m.. For once in my life, I was going to be on time.

58.

On the way home, I picked up a few groceries, in case Cathy would be hungry. I could fix her up a sandwich or something. I even picked up her favourite ice cream. What can I say? I was going to cover all my bases. This was the most important talk of my life coming up.

As I pulled into the driveway, I was puzzled to see not only our other car, but also one that I didn't recognize. The usual media weren't encamped on the street, either. The scene was bizarrely normal. I'd gotten inured to the constant swarming.

The first voice to greet me as I walked in was not Cathy's.

"Donny, Donny, Donny. We finally get our time for a tete-a-tete, you silly sausage, you." Maurice the Magnificent, or whatever he called himself, peered eagerly into my face, rubbing my sleeve ingratiatingly. He mock-scolded me. "You have been impossible to get hold of, you know, and the show is tomorrow!"

Sharon's calm voice came through from the kitchen. "We talked about this, remember, Maurice? Donny was in custody. It was completely out of his control. If he could have, he would have been there for you."

Maurice made a little kissy-mouth of pity for me. "Poor baby. You have been through the wringer. I was in custody once, in Nevada, for something that we're not going to talk about. So I know what you've gone through. Oh, the smells, the lack of privacy, the unkind behaviour of the inmates." He shuddered. "And you don't even get to wear your own clothing. My gawd, those prison outfits are hideous!"

"Maurice, could I make you and Donny a nice pot of tea?" Cathy asked. She was squeezed into the rocking chair, a bemused expression on her face.

My heart jumped up at the sight of her. "Honey, are you OK? Did those creeps hurt you? Is the baby still moving?" I took her hands in mine, probably wringing them a little too passionately, because she winced a little.

"Oh, I'm sorry. I'm just really glad to see you." I dropped her hand in consternation.

Cathy smiled at me but said nothing. She picked up my hand.

"I would absolutely love a cuppa, dear. That is exactly the thing for a weary performer. Earl Grey, please, my sweet. Clear, with a slice of lemon." Maurice apparently did not know that he was not at the Hilton. Before I could respond, Sharon appeared in the entrance to the kitchen.

"Hi, Love," she grinned. "Been in a little trouble, have we? Too bad we can't use this stuff for publicity. It would sell tickets like crazy." She spoke kindly to Cathy. "Stay right there. I'm making the tea. Donny, why don't you and Maurice get started on your ... interview, and then we'll be able to get out of your hair sooner?" She raised her eyebrows significantly.

Maurice had plunked himself down on the sofa and was already patting the cushions beside him. "I have soooo much to ask you. If I am to truly channel Steven, I must know him, inside and out!"

I looked to Cathy apologetically. This was not how our big talk was supposed to go. If I were her, I would be fed up with the endless interruptions. Fortunately for me, Cathy was finding it all rather entertaining.

"Go ahead, Donny, it's important. We can talk later. Maurice is in urgent need of your insights right now."

Maurice excitedly agreed. "That's exactly right! Your insights into the soul of this lost artist named Steven McCartney. Now, I have seen Sharon's collection of photos, but do you have any that I may not have seen?"

I hauled out a photo album that had a few shots here and there of us as young kids. On our bikes, in Stevie's basement, practicing for our band, mugging at the camera at Scout camp. Maurice had become all business. He asked me surprisingly interesting questions about each photo. Had Steven seemed ambitious as a young boy? Did he ever get into fights with other boys?

What was he most likely to get angry about? What was his favourite flavour of Mr. Freeze popsicle treats? And so on.

We moved on to the topic of high school, looking at the old yearbooks.

"What did people like about Steven, do you think?" Maurice asked.

I had often wondered what Steven's secret ingredient was. "Well, I have a few theories," I offered. "He was friendly to everyone, you know, never seemed to treat people disrespectfully. And he was almost always smiling, which people are attracted to, right?" Maurice was nodding thoughtfully, immersed in these ideas. "He charmed the pants off of the girls, but I think that he kinda charmed the guys, too. I'm not too sure how one does that, but he did, I think."

"Was he insincere? Did he deliberately manipulate people, trick them?"

I had thought a lot about that over the years, too. "Maybe sometimes, but we all do. At least, I think that most people do. He wasn't a sleazebag—if he manipulated anyone, it likely wasn't deliberate most of the time."

"What did the girls find so attractive about him?"

This was an easy question to answer. "Well, he was a good-looking guy. Almost no acne, curly hair, blue eyes, athletic, smart as hell—what's not to like?" I thought back to my own awkward, pimpled teen years. Some kids are just born with a get-out-of-hell-free card up their asses, you know?

Maurice looked me in the eyes and asked me the next question with intense directness. "What did you find so attractive about him, Donny? What was it that Steven had that you wanted?"

It was one of those moments of truthfulness where you could try to pretend that the idea had only just occurred to you at that very second, but you know that you've had the answer all along. I had come to a point where lying to myself (or to anyone else, for that matter) was suicide. From now on, it was brutal honesty all the way, baby.

"Well, it's humiliating to say it out loud, but I loved his talent. I craved his talent. All of his talents, but especially the musicianship, the voice. Everything came effortlessly to the guy. I think that I wanted to be him." I took a deep breath. "I was a decent player, but not brilliant. Not a chance of that. Steven, he was brilliant. I think that I'm the only person on this planet who has ever really understood that. Even Steven didn't get that about himself. If he had, he never would have betrayed his gift by walking away from it like that." I was shocked to hear the bitterness creeping into my own voice. How could I still be holding onto that feeling, a whole lifetime later?

Maurice the Miraculous (I never could remember his self-assigned titles) sighed back down into the sofa cushions, looking positively sated. "My darling man, I cannot tell you how old this tale is. It has been so since mankind first sang songs." He gazed at me with compassion. "You absolutely must not beat yourself up about these feelings anymore. Of course you wanted to have the Voice! Who wouldn't? Is anyone honestly going to stand before the Creator and say "Sorry, great talent just doesn't interest me. Do you have any mediocrity lying about that you could give me?!" Oh!" he huffed. "The ability to express the music that dwells inside of each of us—the God-given music of the universe, darling—well, it's sublime. It is the most satisfying feeling that a human being is capable of having. And it is entirely forgivable and natural to wish that you had it! I ought to know." And on that note he ended his remarkable sermon.

Cathy was staring in awe at Maurice, a half-grin on her face. Sharon was leaning against the doorframe in the kitchen, looking completely unfazed by all of this. "Tea's ready, Maurice. You must be thirsty after all that talking."

Maurice looked a little miffed that his eloquent speech had been labelled as mere "talking", but Sharon waved a plate of chocolate-covered Peek Frean biscuits in front of his nose and he immediately headed for the tea set up on the kitchen table. Sharon smirked at us behind his back. "Thank God for cookies," she whispered.

I sat there for a few moments in silence. Maurice's words had penetrated to the core of me. He was right. Right on the money. How could I ever have predicted that today I would be receiving absolution for my sins from Pope Peacock? And that it would genuinely effect me like this?

I must have looked pretty stunned, because when I finally looked over at Cathy, she said, "Are you gonna be OK?" She came over and sat down beside me. A little smile played around the corners of her mouth. We just sat there, holding hands in silence and looking into each others' eyes, as corny as that may sound.

Sharon, God bless her, must have been psychic, because I heard her cajoling Maurice away from the remaining cookies and out of the kitchen.

" And you don't want to put on any pounds, right? That cute little tush of yours is a professional asset, no pun intended. Now, let's get you back to the hotel for a little rest before tonight's rehearsal." She playfully patted his rear end and winked at us as they sailed out.

"Sweetheart, I am flattered, but I don't swing that way, and let me tell you, even Elton himself couldn't get a piece of me until after this concert," Maurice said, giggling. "Farewell, Donny my Love! See you tomorrow!" he called out behind him.

"I think that he likes you," Cathy said, straight-faced. "I guess that I may have a little competition on my hands. And he does have a great tush."

I suddenly felt the tears in my eyes. I never cried. Cathy was the one who had a heart; she had always seemed to have some extra degree of compassion that I was missing. During movies, I would gauge the sadness of a scene by whether or not she was wiping tears from her eyes. And now I was the one wiping my eyes, and Cathy was looking at me, dry-eyed.

I opened my mouth to speak, but a weird little squeak came out. Embarrassment drained my veins. I was afraid of the power of my emotions—always had been—but I knew I had to let them out this time, even if it killed me.

59.

Cathy's gaze hadn't faltered since Maurice and Sharon had left. She wouldn't take her eyes off mine. I jumped in, desperate.

"You know, Cathy," I said, "that I love you." Her silent, serious eyes said *yes*. I put a trembling arm around her shoulders and squeezed in closer to her on the couch. "You're the love of my life. You always have been and you always will be. But I see it now—I'm selfish. And I have a big ego." I cleared my throat. "I'm really sorry for running us all over the place for all these years. I've ruined some of your best years, and that's not right. I guess I ... I've always focussed my attention on what I *don't* have. As if Life owes me something more. I've wasted my life, just ignoring how much I already have, what a lucky guy I really am. I wish to God I'd seen this earlier, but I guess I had to truly bottom out before I could change." Cathy quietly passed me a Kleenex so that I could blow my nose. It was starting to get easier, this opening up of my soul business. "I also don't want to lie ever again, Cath, and I'm through chasing fame—it sucks, I hate it, and I *hate* myself for ever wanting something that shallow. It's *not* important—I can see that now, clearly." Cathy was stroking my leg, a sad little smile on her face. "I wouldn't blame you for not believing me when I say that, Cath. I wouldn't blame you." My voice was trailing off. I pulled her into my arm and cried like a newborn baby—there, now it's said. Now you know. And I said it, and normally I would never say that kind of thing to anyone, so I really had changed, and it's a big relief, let me tell you.

We were both crying, and I whispered a promise to Cathy. I meant it more deeply than any promise I'd ever made to her.

"You know how I knew I still loved you?" she said, her face muffled against my shirt.

I shook my head, unable to speak.

"When those American agents forced you into their car and drove away. My heart just split open for you, Donny. It was a physical pain." There was still a note of surprise in her voice. "I wanted my Donny back, my partner for life! It's like we're Siamese twins—I felt torn in half when they took you. And it really hit me that I needed you. Despite your flaws," she added mischievously.

"I guess it takes a terrible crisis for two people to truly realize that," I said.

She smiled up at me. "For these two people, anyway."

We stayed that way a long time. Other than the experience of seeing my child born in the delivery room, I don't think I've had a moment more poignant. I saw, for the first time, how really lucky I was to be married to Cathy.

60.

Saturday, October 5.
10:00 a.m.

The problem with make-up sex is that it isn't sex at all. It's too powerfully charged with sadness and love and a million other feelings to be just good, normal sex. By the time it's over, you feel like you've just had an enema for the emotions. So, when we woke up the next morning, neither of us felt quite on the ball. But I must say that I felt relief so intense that it was painful when I woke up to feel my wife beside me again. Cathy's hair looked like half a beehive, and she had morning breath, and she had to manoeuvre her belly like a beached whale to get out of bed, but she was radiating beauty, as far as I was concerned.

"Do you want coffee or tea, hon?" she asked as she shuffled toward the kitchen. *I have someone who actually wants to make me a cup of tea!* I thought happily. *First thing in the morning, and she thinks of me!* I floated on a wave of gratitude for a moment.

"Cath, I am going to make breakfast. You sit down and read the paper, drink your OJ, relax. Do you want easy-over or scrambled?" Cathy smiled shyly at me. Clearly, she was pleased. *I've got to do this more often,* I thought, *put Cathy first, even if it's just a little thing.*

The Saturday paper was late, so Cathy read me the disturbing bits of the news from Friday's paper while I put on the meal. "I haven't seen the paper in a couple of days, so it's still fresh news to me," she said cheerfully. When she got to the Entertainment Section, she went silent. My heart went cold when I realized why. She was reading my column. *Oh God,* I prayed, *please don't let that stupid column ruin all the progress we've made.* This fragile, beautiful reunion of ours had to be cherished, protected. I stood at the stove, back to her, afraid to breathe. I couldn't think of any words to say that would help.

Then I felt two warm, soft arms wrap around my middle. Cathy laid her head against my back and said, "I do love you." A woman's capacity to love a seriously flawed, perhaps even hopelessly demented man has always astounded me. And I am bloody grateful for it.

I turned around to embrace her, passion pounding through my body. Cathy's arms were surprisingly powerful. As we squeezed each other into oblivion, I suddenly felt a thud against my stomach.

"The baby just kicked me!" I cried out in delight. "Oh my God! He's so strong!" An overwhelming wave of reality swept over me. "Oh my goodness. I have to sit down, honey. Just sit down with me, OK?" I felt weak and out of breath.

Cathy eyed me with a half-smile on her face. "It's pretty amazing, isn't it? There's a living person inside of me. It's a miracle." Her voice was quiet and calming.

The sense of awe stayed with me for some time that morning. So this was what women felt when they carried around a new life. A baby wasn't just imagination, or a bunch of cells that wasn't a person until you could see it in a bassinette—our child was real, alive and kicking, as they say, right now. Cathy was already a mother. And I was already a father.

I'm a father. I have a child.

The thought was universe-shifting.

61.

The Steven McCartney Story: The Final Column.
by Donny Love

Let me share with all of you a message from Steven. He has been following some of the media brouhaha over his life story, and he feels that it is urgent that he set the record straight.

First of all, Steven wants you to know that some of the stories about him circulating in the media are sheer nonsense. He hopes that you will apply your good sense to your understanding of these tall tales. Even I, who have a bond of friendship spanning decades with this man, am not privy to all of the mysteries of his very private life.

Secondly, Steven has never been interested in gaining celebrity or wealth. He has said that our purpose in this life is to help others, to love, to forgive, and to spread wisdom. He begs each of you to do the same. Imagine what kind of world we could create with that sense of purpose.

Finally, Steven has sworn to me that his performance at this weekend's gala concert at Irondale Collegiate will be his last public appearance. He has found that the recent blast of obsessive attention from the public and the media has seriously hindered him in his life's work of helping others. At the end of the concert, he will disappear from the public eye and go back to living in the seclusion that he so loves. There will be no interviews. There will be no more columns.

We will have to become heroes ourselves. Each of us.

62.

Cathy's reaction to the column was to love me even more. Alas, that was not the case with a lot of other people.

The reaction to the column from Steven's fans was, in a word, ugly.

I had missed the initial furor on Friday, being caught up in Maurice's web, but Bob had left several strange messages on my voice mail. When I finally got around to listening to them on Saturday morning, I was alarmed.

Message number 1: "Chamberlain here, Love. Just wanted you to know that today's column is getting ... mixed reviews, you could say. From a writing standpoint, it's the best yet. Really. But there's a problem with upper management. They feel that you should not have ended this series without their OK ... Shit, let's be honest, Love. That column has been the only thing selling this paper for the past three weeks, and those fuckers upstairs know that they're screwed now. Just call me. I need a bone to throw them."

Message number 2: "Love, if you're thinking of coming in today, forget it. In fact, you should probably hole up at a friend's house and keep your head down for awhile. There's a bunch of crazy freaks outside the *Gazette*, and ten to one they'll try to gather outside your house, too. Just lie low. And call me."

Message number 3: "Donny, I hope to God that those whack-jobs haven't got their hands on you. If you're alive and well, you'd better call me right now, boy, because I'm getting a little concerned, OK? (At that moment, his voice became muffled, as he covered the receiver.) They did what? Are you shitting me, Meg? Goddamn it! Call Allan Hill. Bunch of psychos! (He came back onto the line) Sorry about that! Little problem here. Just stay the hell away from here, Donny, and wear a wig and sunglasses or something, OK? And call me!"

Cathy heard the last message as she came out of the shower. "Donny, what was that? Oh my gosh, it sounds like someone's after you. A wig and sunglasses?" Her face was tight with worry. At that moment, we heard a commotion outside the house. I opened the door to find our paper delivery man shouting angrily at a group of strangers lining our sidewalk.

"What the hell, man? Can't you just let a guy do his job? Ya moron!" The poor guy turned to put the paper in my mailbox. The sight of me standing there just about gave him a heart attack. He handed me the thick bundle of newsprint and eyed me balefully. "Some people are just ignorant," he muttered. As he turned to break through the crowd again, he yelled at all of them.

"You'd better get the hell outta my way, cause I'm not going around ya! Move!"

In a state of shock, Cathy and I hurriedly shut the door, breathing fast. Leaning against it as I locked the deadbolt, the sounds of booing and general unhappiness filtered through. I dropped to my hands and knees and carefully scuttled over to the window. Cathy was fast on my heels.

"Who are these people? What do they want?" she hissed.

"They want Steven. And they wanna get me for taking him away from them," I muttered. We edged the window blind open and peeked out. It was scary out there. At least 30 people were assembled on the sidewalk. Some had placards (*Come back, Steven!*, *Where is the Love for McCartney?*, and *Give me my Steven!* were the most notable). There were a number wearing Steven T-shirts, buttons, etc. One person was dangling an effigy from a noose. I really hoped that that was not supposed to be me.

Cathy's sharp intake of breath behind me told me that she had seen the effigy, too. She gripped my leg tightly. "Call the police!" she whispered. "Call 911 right now!"

No sooner had she said the words than we heard sirens coming up the street. Two cop cars pulled up beside the crowd. God bless our pernickety neighbours. The police were having a hard time getting people to leave peacefully. After one officer found himself wrestling with a woman in her 60's, they called for back-up. It took four cop cars and 45 minutes more to clear the area. When they were done, two of the harried-looking officers came up the walkway to the door.

When Cathy opened it and they caught sight of her big tummy, the expressions on their faces softened a bit.

"Ma'am, Sir, I am Constable Sawicki and this is Constable Arnold. There has been a disturbance outside your home this morning. Did you see it?"

I nodded. "Sorry, Officer. I think that they're angry about the column that I write."

Constable Arnold peered at me suddenly. "Are you the guy who writes about Steven McCartney?"

I nodded again nervously.

Constable Arnold was quickly returning to his professionally impassive face, but he muttered quietly, "I love that guy."

The officers warned us that they couldn't stand guard outside the house, so that the best thing for us to do would be to stay with a friend or family member, and to do it soon, before the crowd began to trickle back. We thanked them and hurried to pack an overnight bag.

"Who should we stay with?" Cathy asked.

"Cath, I think that we'll have to go to Mum and Dad's. They'll be really hurt if they hear that we went anywhere else in our hour of need." I smiled at her apologetically.

She gave me one of her Marge Simpson grumbles of disapproval, but she gave in. "Just don't let your Dad smoke in the house." She rubbed her stomach. "The baby, right?"

We sneaked out the back door, and Cathy hid at the side of the house until I had her car door unlocked and the engine running. She held her belly as she dashed to the car, hurling her bulk onto the seat.

"Be careful, honey!" I cried. "Take it easy. I don't want you *or* the baby to get hurt!" Cathy's response was to madly stretch her arms across me to lock my door. You'd think that we were trying to escape flesh-eating zombies.

I squealed the tires a little bit on the way out of the driveway.

I couldn't help myself.

63.

As we stepped through the front door of my parent's vault, the waft of sizzling bacon and eggs permeated the air. Saturday is breakfast for lunch, I remembered. The sound of bagpipes shook the glassware in the china cabinet. Music from the classic record album, *Auld Reekie Scottish Dance Band*. I'd been raised on that music.

We had stopped at Opie's Bakery on Concession Street to pick up some Scottish baps. The boy inside me needed to come here and feel a piece of home.

"How are you doing, Mum?" I called from the hallway. We slipped off our shoes.

Mum's tired voice came from the kitchen. "Not good."

Cathy and I looked at each other in consternation. My folks were at the age where their health was precarious, at best.

"What's wrong?" I asked, walking up the three steps from the hallway and into the kitchen. Mum stood leaning on a walker next to the stove, a pan of sizzling bacon in one hand. "Mum, what are you doing out of bed? It's too hard on your knees, let Dad cook the lunch."

She scowled and shook her head. "He's at it again."

"What?" asked Cathy, innocently.

I put my hand on Mum's shoulder and passed a quick look of warning to Cathy. "I'll go down and see him, OK, Mum?" I skillfully distracted my Mum from her worries about Dad. "Cath, why don't you put your feet up? You need to rest, honey. Mum, do you have a glass of milk for Cathy?"

My mother sprang into action. She would certainly never let her pregnant daughter-in-law want for anything while under her roof. As I headed into the basement, I heard Mum quizzing Cathy about the crazies outside our house. Cathy was careful to mention nothing about our recent separation and reunion.

The old teenager feelings of shame and anger flooded back, as I headed down the steps towards Dad's secret lair, coined "the inner sanctum" by Mum, a room under the stairs. Ducking down because of the five-foot ceiling, I could see the top of Dad's head behind the layers of criss-crossing strings where he'd clothes pinned dead lottery tickets. Inside was thick blue cigarette smoke, an old beige carpet full of cigarette burns, and a dilapidated old oak desk stacked with hundreds of lottery tickets that Dad had labelled with strange, secretive markings, dating as far back as the seventies.

"Dad? How's the Breaking of the Code going?" I hesitantly asked.

He sat up from his desk, and pulled down a string of tickets so he could see me over it. He humphed and then let go of the string, the tickets bobbing up and down. His face was mostly hidden again.

I decided to try again. "Dad, how about leaving this for now? It's unhealthy as hell down here—all this smoke and darkness. Come on upstairs and we'll have a cuppa on the deck. Okay?" Typically, there was no response. That sort of thing had frustrated me all of my life.

Dad had a big head. He wore the same thick-lensed glasses that he'd had in the sixties. He'd been folically challenged from day one, but there were still some tufts of fading red hair above his ears. An Export A' cigarette stuck to his lip like an appendage, darting in and out of his mouth as he spoke. On the floor around him, empty McEwans beer cans littered the floor. A 1972 calendar from back *hame* in Scotland was still pinned to a wall stud.

"So, are you getting close, Dad?"

"Blether, blether, you're still a windbag, son. And I know why you're down here." He continued to tinker away, not even bothering to look up.

"Dad, you've been at this for years, but you've never won the jackpot. What makes you still think you're going to crack the Code?"

Dad's jaw went up in defiance."What makes you think I won't? I'm getting closer every year.

I have predicted seven wins over the years." Dad didn't go on to mention that he had blown his own system by forgetting to buy the tickets on those seven occasions. It was too bitter a memory.

"Dad, it's all random. There's no skill in it." In our house, this sort of talk was considered heresy.

"*Weesht*, man. You're brainwashed, Donny. There's fixes in all things, including sports. Why, there's the trots, the slots, and lottery tickets. You know as well as I do the casinos program their slot machines to pay out every so many pulls of the lever."

He pushed past me and went over to the old Sears stereo console, searching the collection of LPs and pulling out a record. "Sergio Mendez—brilliant! Why don't you write about him in your column, Donny? That man was an underrated genius."

"Or write about the crazy old Scot trying to crack the lottery code," I said, under my breath.

"I heard that, Sonny Jim! Bite your tongue, or I'll bash out your teeth." That was the sort of affectionate talk that I had grown up with. Charming. I made a mental note to myself to never threaten to bash out my child's teeth.

"Anyway, you're one to talk. That rubbish column of yours! Pah! What the hell did that lazy bastard Steven McCartney ever offer the world? He was no good in the day when you were chummin' with him. Another one of your Eddie

Hascal buddies, all nice as pie on the outside but phoney inside. Should've given them all a Glasgow kiss when I had the chance."

Since Dad was in a mean mood, I decided to jolly him up. I put on the Sergio Mendez album.

In an instant mood change (one of the things that always astounded me about him), he danced and shimmied, snapping his fingers. My fondest memories of childhood were the dance parties on New Year's Eve that he and Mum had held in our basement.

I looked around the old wood-panelled basement, and at the black marks on the door where I used to drill hockey pucks. The dart board, ping-pong table, the old stereo. Everything was still there. But my folks hadn't had a party down here in 10 years. Water stains marked some of the ceiling tiles. On the window sill, spiders had strung webs between the bowling trophies. Everything seemed so small to me now. I'd turned these memories over in my mind one too many times, and doing that had sucked the magic out of them. Now, standing here, the basement seemed a dead place.

Sighing deeply, I noticed that the window and door were wired. Attached to the wires was a huge megaphone.

"I like your new security device," I said, trying to sound positive.

"Aye, I'm ready for the intruders now," Dad said. He started to puff a little bit from the exertion of his dancing. "Ach, I don't have the wind I used to, lad. Age doesn't come by itself." He turned to me. "I never said this, son, but I'm glad you don't smoke. It's a killer."

I nodded. I'd tried in the past to get him to quit, but he'd just go inward and not say a peep. When Mum would berate him for it, he'd slip out to his garage-cave to get away from her and smoke his brains out. Smoking was not only a physical addiction for Dad, but a highly emotional one, as well. I imagined that it kept Dad's demons at bay. The demon thing seemed to run in the family.

He slung his arm around me, still panting. "I don't like to tell you how to run your life, son, but maybe you're not meant to be a columnist. When you were a lad you were a great organizer, you know. You could whip together a hockey game on a dime, and you were a Sixer in Scouts. Not only that, but you were captain of your house league hockey team. I always saw you in a management-type job, Donny. When you're ready to come down from the clouds, you can settle down and find yourself a real job. Crack the whip, Donny." He shook a fist in the air. "Aye, here comes Donny Love, get crackin' everyone!" He laughed and wheezed.

Ah, it was the same old message of disapproval of my choices in life. The only thing that I'd ever done that my parents approved of wholeheartedly was to marry Cathy. I had long since given up trying to defend myself in these moments. "We'll see, Dad."

"Care for a beer?"

I grimaced. "It's a little early, Dad."

"Enough with the faces, son—it's Scottish beer. You can drink that any time of day."

Jesus, you're so hardcore.

With great stealth, Dad placed two cans of McEwans on the tikki bar. As he always did when he wanted to keep his basement shenanigans to himself, he covered up his beer cracking sounds by singing *The Bonnie Banks of O' Loch Lomond*. Mum knew his old trick, and if you were upstairs and he started singing, she would shake her head, scowl, and make her trademark gasping sound.

"I heard that Archie!" Mum called down sharply.

"Right, get to it, son, before the auld lady pulls the plug on our party."

"Right, it's out!" Mum called from the top of the stairs, the bacon and eggs aroma reaching us.

"Coming, Mother, coming!" Dad said. "Ach, cut short again," he muttered. He tipped the beer to his mouth and drank the contents in three gorging swallows.

Always impatient, Mum called down again. "Hurry up before it gets cold!"

"We heard you the first time, woman!" Dad cried, his face turning red. "Now *wheesht*!" He turned to me with a wink. "It's a good thing I'm not a violent man." And up we went, as ordered.

64.

"I can't believe you've kept those, Mum."

We were sitting around, nursing our tea, breakfast finished.

She was very matter-of-fact, as usual. "Well, even though the content was rubbish, not fit for the bing, really, they were well-written."

From my Mum, this was a compliment. "Thanks, Mum."

My Dad piped in with his two cents' worth. "That McCartney's the reincarnation of Eddie Hascal. I wouldn't write about him if my life depended on it." He slurped his coffee loudly.

My mother responded sharply. "Aye, well no one's asking you to, Archie."

"Blether, blether, blether." He adjusted his glasses.

This was the comfortable pattern of their conversations. When I had first brought Cathy home for dinners, she had been very upset by the arguing and raising of voices, but now it was old hat to her, too. "Esme, can I get you another cup of tea?" she asked sweetly.

Mum had put all of my Steven columns up on the fridge.

"Donny, you're almost as famous now as Steven," Mum said.

Again, Dad had to insert his opinion. His voice was bitter. "Steven McCartney's no' famous. He'll end up in jail with Donny once this is all over."

"He'll not!" Mom responded angrily. "I'd be so lucky if you went to jail, Archie!" She turned back to me as if nothing had happened. "I bought tickets for the show. Your Dad and I will be going."

"Aye, I'll be going, pissed out of my mind."

"Shut it, Archie."

"Are you sure you want to come? What if Steven doesn't show?" I asked.

My Dad loved that one. "Accchh, that pimply-faced weasel won't show."

"Dad, why do you suddenly hate Steven so much? What has he ever done to you, or to anyone, for that matter? I'm the one who's done the damage here. You should probably hate me." I felt a sick wave of shame again. Cathy put her hand on top of mine reassuringly.

Dad was not in the mood for analysing his feelings. That sort of thing was definitely not in his genetic make-up. He growled, "I'm just sayin' that if I see that McCartney boy I'll break his bloody face." My mother's eyebrows went up as prelude to another blow-out.

Cathy intervened again. "How about I freshen up your tea, Archie? And would you like another slice of toast?" Dad's mood suddenly changed. Tea is like mother's milk to a Scot, I think.

"Yeah, and some o'that nice blackberry jam wi'that, Cathy. That's good stuff, that." He leaned conspiratorially over to me as Cathy headed over to the stove. "Cathy's putting on a bit o' weight round her belly, son. Time to cut back on they sandwiches."

Mum stared in shock at Dad. "You old fool, she's pregnant! Eight months! Did you not listen to any of the hundreds of conversations that we had about this all year?" She scowled in disgust. She'd finally had enough, hobbling over to the TV, where I heard the football match between the Celtics and the Rangers come on. Her tone immediately changed. "Oh, oh, Archie! It's the big game! Come on, Rangers! Kick their arses! Come on, Arch! You're goin' to miss it!"

And just like that, my Dad and Mum were a team again, united in their love of the Rangers, temporarily in a truce. Dad shuffled quickly into his Lazy Boy armchair, tea slopping out of his cup. Cathy and I could have had wild sex right there on the table and they wouldn't have noticed. Some things never change.

But sometimes people do.

With all of the painful changes wrought in me over the past weeks, I realized that there was now one more to add to the list: I was a grown-up, fully, truly, irreversibly, in a way that I had never felt before.

You know how annoying it is when you are a young adult, holding down a job, living on your own, fully independent, and then a married friend with a child says something or does something that makes you feel like the frivolous kid in the group? I knew that feeling well. But now I suddenly got it. Now I was the guy with the ultimate responsibility, the ultimate path to growth in life. I was a dad. And even if there was some kind of going back, I did not want to. I was no longer my parents' wayward child. I was a man.

I looked at my parents, who were completely under the spell of Scottish football, and felt ... detached. Not lacking in love for them, just fully separated. It didn't matter to me anymore whether they approved or disapproved of my choices. I didn't need them for comfort or safety. I didn't feel any more anger, resentment, or shame about them. I was just glad that they were in this world, and that I could share some time with them.

I felt a warm arm slip around my shoulders. Cathy was smiling meaningfully at me."Let's go upstairs," she whispered. "I have something to show you. I think that my breasts have grown another cup size." She always did know how to sweet-talk me.

65.

During a break in the big game, Mum changed channels to see a bit of the news.

"Donny!" she cried. "Get down here and see this! Your show is on the CBC news!"

The concert! I had forgotten about it, and, believe me, that had been a welcome oblivion. Filled with dread, I quickly tidied myself up and joined my parents in the living room. The CBC anchor woman was explaining to the rest of Canada who Steven McCartney was and how he had come to be booked for a small but wildly popular concert in Hamilton, Ontario, of all places.

"Few could have predicted the impact on Hamilton's economy when local entertainment columnist Donny Love began a series of articles on his old childhood friend. Today, there is a booming industry in Hamilton and elsewhere for Steven McCartney paraphernalia. Tickets for tonight's concert have been estimated to have a street value of at least 400 dollars Canadian, which is remarkable, considering that the venue is a high school auditorium. McCartney is a mystery, without a recording to his name, yet his popularity has soared in the past few weeks, as Hollywood has jumped on the Steven McCartney bandwagon. Several red carpet celebrities from

Los Angeles will be in the audience tonight, to cheer for this iconic hero. Michael Vareau has more as he reports to us from Hamilton."

The mention of Hollywood stars at the concert stopped my heart. Who? Was this a publicity thing staged by Sharon? Or had people in Hollywood really swallowed this fantasy? This was getting way too big, but there was nothing that I could do. I thought of the rehearsal with Maurice—I still had no idea if he could even sing—and my stomach heaved.

"Honey, are you feeling alright? You look awful." Cathy had joined us in front of the TV and was staring at me concernedly.

"I just need the bathroom," I said breathlessly. I hurried over to my Mum's pink and gold main floor powder room.

"Donny, now that room's for guests, remember!" my Mum called out after me. "Don't be leaving a mess of my towels!"

As I hovered over the toilet, stomach churning, I could hear much of the broadcast through the door.

"Oh my goodness!" Cathy cried out to me through the bathroom door. "Did you know that Pam Anderson is coming tonight, Donny?" There was a pause. "And Brad Pitt! Brad Pitt!" I could hear her trying to calm her voice for my sake. Then I heard shrieking from Cathy and whoops from my folks. "Paul McCartney! Oh my God! Paul McCartney! AAAAAH!"

There may have been other stars mentioned, but I was beyond hearing them. I vomited violently for several minutes. Cathy knocked softly on the door and came in. She bent over me, putting a motherly hand on my back and handing me wads of toilet paper. Nothing says "I love you" like staying with someone while he pukes his guts out.

When I had finished, Cathy helped me to sit on the toilet lid and calm myself. My hands and legs were still shaking. I opened my mouth to say something, but Cathy beat me to it.

"Donny, I want to say a few things to you. First of all, I know that you're terrified about tonight, but try not to be. Whatever happens will happen. I don't know if we'll be sued, or if there are criminal charges that could be laid against you. I don't know if you'll still have your job. Maybe we'll have to flee the country. I don't know." (At this point, I was feeling terribly reassured. That Cathy knew how to drive a nail home.) "I do know that, whatever happens, I'll be there with you, and our marriage will withstand whatever horrible circumstances might arise."

I stared at Cathy, not sure whether to wail in panic or laugh.

"Secondly, whatever happens as a result of this column and this concert doesn't even matter. It doesn't, Donny. What matters is our family—you, me, and our little baby." She rubbed her tummy lovingly. "Just keep reminding yourself, honey: all that matters in this life is your relationships with the people who love you." She smiled beatifically at me. Was that a light glowing behind her head? I felt like I was watching the last few minutes of an episode of *Touched By An Angel*.

"Okay, last thing I want to say, and then the sermon will end." She suddenly jerked with a suppressed giggle. "Would you *pul-eeze introduce me to Brad Pitt?*"

My Dad grumpily called out,"What's goin' on in there?", at the sound of Cathy's peals of laughter.

66.

Sharon called at 5:00 pm.

"Where the hell have you been, Love? I've been trying to reach you all afternoon!" She sounded frazzled and just a little bit panicked, which did nothing for my own anxiety level. Sharon was always calm under pressure, so I quaked at the thought of how bad things must be.

"Okay, Sharon, just break it to me gently, okay?" My voice cracked a little bit. *Great! Donny hits puberty on the night of the big concert, while the world watches. Fucking great!* I thought angrily. "How bad is he? I mean, do you think that they'll want their money back? Can we even do that?"

There was a hubbub on the other end. Sharon was talking to someone. "*Money back? What do you mean? Hank! I heard. Where? Did you kick them out? Okay, I want to see at least 10 extra security guards here. I don't care. Call them in. Of course we've got the budget! You get me more security here in the next half hour, Caveman, and leave the higher levels of thinking to me, right?*" She puffed out an angry stream of breath. "What, Donny? I'm just dealing with some stuff here. Didn't hear you. *Not over there, guys! We revised the staging an hour ago. Go see Jeff for the diagrams.* Donny? Look, I can't talk. I just wanted you to see this. You won't believe it. Oh, and remember that you and your family and friends are on the backstage list, so go around to the back and come in through the stage entrance after the show. *What? Shit! I told you not to talk to him before the performance. Now I'm going to have to calm him down all over again. Shit!* Gotta go, Donny! Get over here soon!" And with that, Sharon hung up.

"We have to get over there soon," I said numbly to Cathy. I felt like I was walking to the guillotine. There would be a crowd there, thirsty for my blood.

We quickly ate a bowl of soup and a sandwich. I think that I was on autopilot, because I was surprised to look down and see that I had eaten. Cathy had to remind me to put my shoes on before we left. Mum and Dad were watching more Scottish football and seemed not to have noticed my state. Cathy reminded them to come around to the backstage entrance afterward and to come over to the show a bit early.

"Because the crowds might be a bit big," she said.

Just as we were opening the front door, the phone rang again.

67.

"For you, Donny," Dad called out from the living room.

I stopped at the door. "For me?" *I really don't have time for this. Probably some telemarketer tracked me down to my parents' house.* I turned at the open door and headed back into the living room and the land of football.

"Who is it?" I asked.

"Alvin the Chipmunk. How should I know?" he snapped.

Dad, seemingly oblivious to me, held the phone out in the air while he kept his gaze fixed on the soccer match. "Don't give out your credit card number, Donny. Probably some wee freak sitting in his undies in his sordid little apartment trying to sell you a bogus vacation for two. Oh aye, yours is free, but your wife has to pay 300 dollars if she wants to go. Bullshite! Any man like that should have his bloody heed cut off."

I grabbed the phone from the old gibbering fool. "Hello?"

"Donny?" a familiar voice asked through a haze of static.

"Speaking," I said, tentatively.

"It's Steven McCartney, man."

A hot burning shiver dripped down my back. A numbness grew inside my head. "Steven?" I managed. "Steven McCartney?" My throat felt tight.

"Yeah, your old friend."

"Steven, I ... I thought you were dead, man! I haven't heard from you in so long, I really thought you were dead, I was afraid you were dead." I was starting to hyperventilate, and I had to lean against the wall beside the coffee table to steady myself. My legs were threatening to buckle. My folks and Cathy looked alarmed.

"I'm alive and kicking," he said. "I can't believe that I got you at your folks' house. And I can't believe that I still remembered your old phone number after all these years. After all those years of calling you, I think it's still hard-wired in my brain, that and my old school locker combination." He laughed.

His voice sounded higher than I remembered. Like the old man said, he sounded a little bit like a chipmunk, almost as if his voice hadn't changed since high school. A wash of static threatened the connection.

"Where are you, Steven? What happened? We—" I'd barely spoken the word when a sound like a throttling truck engine blared through the phone.

"Pardon?" he said. "Sorry, it's really loud here. I told them to give me five minutes. Can never get any peace around this damn place." He laughed ruefully.

"Is that that Steven McCartney on the phone?" Dad said, "What's he onto now, telemarketing scams?"

"Dad, shut up," I said. "Once and for all, just shut up."

He didn't flinch, his gaze unmoving from the television. He turned up the volume a notch just to show me he was pissed at me. *Fuck you, too, Dad!*

"Your Dad hasn't changed a bit," Steven said. "Still the crotchety Scotsman."

"What about your parents?" I asked. I raised my voice to be heard above the cacophony through Steven's end of the phone.

"They're dead, Donny. Dad died a few years ago, and Mom followed six months later. I think she just couldn't live without him. You hear about that stuff all the time."

"Man, I'm sorry," I said. I felt so stupid. Of course they were dead. We already knew that. My brain wasn't in gear for this phonecall.

"Thanks. That's how it goes, right? But I really miss them sometimes."

I swallowed—hearing about his parents hurt me. My own parents were next in line. There were more loud sounds on the other end—people barking orders, a child crying. "Where the hell are you, Steven? It sounds like the movie soundtrack to *Evil Dead*."

I thought he'd find that funny, but he didn't.

"I'm in Darfur. I'm an aid worker. Been here about nine years, but I did similar stuff in other places before that. Just kinda fell into it, you know?"

"Wow," I said, feeling very juvenile for trying to crack my *Evil Dead* joke. I tried to swallow the lump the size of a golf ball that sat in my throat.

"Life's full of twists and turns, eh, Donny? I mean, who knew where any of us would end up after high school?"

I sure hadn't, apparently. "Are you married? Do you have kids?" I asked.

"Yep, for 10 years. I have a son, Callum. He's six. He and Nyarai don't live here with me, though. Too dangerous. I go visit them in Kenya on my leaves. That part's pretty hard, not being with them." I could hear the change in his voice.

"I have one, too. Well, on the way. We don't know if it's a boy or a girl." I thought about how I would feel, limited to seeing my wife and child once every few months.

Everything I'd planned to say if I saw or spoke to Steven again had long since vanished from my brain. A vague feeling that he'd known since Grade 12 what was important began to rise inside me. *Steven grew up years ago, Donny, unlike you. He got it, even then. He's spent his adult life helping people, risking himself for others. That last column was more right than you could have known.*

Steven was speaking very loudly to be heard over the din around him. "Listen, I heard about your columns from another Canadian out here, a UN peacekeeper. The guy calls me Clint. He says you've been making me out to be some kinda hero? And now I'm supposedly a rock star or something? I don't understand it, to be honest, but I thought I'd give you a call. What the hell, it's been such a long time, right?"

"Oh yeah, the columns, I'm sor—"

"—So you're a journalist now." I could imagine him grinning a mile wide. I was thrown off a bit by not being able to offer my much-dreaded apology. Steven didn't seem to have cared too much. "I pictured you playing in the world's biggest rock band, Donny!"

"Yeah, I know, but I got over that a long time ago," I lied. *A week ago to be exact!* I felt stunted, as if I'd lived in a horrible time warp for the last twenty years, searching for rock'n'roll fame.

"Aw, you always had the talent and the drive for it, man. Seriously."

This was a shocker. "N-no, you were the guy, Steven. You had it, man. The—the golden touch." It felt ridiculous to be stating the obvious to him like this. Didn't he recognize his own talent?

Steven snorted derisively. "Aw, I never saw any of that." He said something to someone who was talking to him. "So, it sounds like there's going to be quite a concert tonight, buddy. How the hell did you arrange that?"

I felt a stabbing sensation in my heart, and I paused, waiting for him to blast me.

Silence.

"I hired an impersonator," I said meekly.

"What the hell? Who in their right mind would want to impersonate *me*?" He was laughing on the other end of the phone. "Donny, man, the only Steven McCartney you knew was that show-off kid from high school. What's worth impersonating there?"

Steven's laughter suddenly freed me to say what I needed to say to my old friend, this stranger. "Listen, I'm really sorry about writing that bullshit about you. To be honest, I missed you. I missed the excitement of you and I rockin' out—just sailing on that feeling that anything could happen, that we could make it big someday. I grew up, Steven, but my dreams didn't." Even I could hear the bitterness in my voice." And ever since, Donny Love has been chasing his youth, and here I am almost 40, married, expecting a child. You've been saving people, Stevie, but I've wasted half my life, man. How's that for blind!"

Steven apparently didn't find me as contemptible as I found myself. He responded by singing lyrics into the phone: "*That deaf, dumb, and blind kid sure plays a mean pinball!*" In Grade 11 we'd performed bits of The Who's *Tommy* at the Irondale Variety Night. "Donny, take it easy, brother. You're still a young man. You have your whole life ahead of you. There's lots of time to get your life right. And I'm no saint, okay? Lots of people do what I do, and lots do even more than I do, so don't put me up on some kinda pedestal, OK?" He sounded serious, almost stern.

A wash of static flooded the phone line.

"Steven? Are you still there?"

"Yeah, I'm still here."

I felt myself on the verge of tears, but held it together. "Steven, to be honest, you and the other guys were the only real friends I ever had."

Steven sighed heavily. "Donny, you're still my friend."

"Yeah?"

"Of course. Do you still live in The Hammer?"

"Yeah, we moved back here not too long ago."

"Good, I'll look you up the next time I'm through. I'm thinking of coming back over Christmas to show Callum Canada. He's never been outside of this region. The poor kid thinks that everybody in the world carries automatic rifles. We'll get together then, OK?"

"Hey, that would be awesome."

More static, thicker and louder this time.

"Anyway, Donny, good luck at the show tonight. I hope this Steven guy rocks the place." He laughed again. What a good sound that was!

"That makes two of us."

"I better be—"

"—Steven?"

"Yeah?"

"Do you forgive me for writing the columns?"

A pause. "That all depends on how well I perform at the show tonight. I have my reputation to keep up. Bye, buddy. Be good."

I smiled. "So long, Steven. Take care of yourself."

On my left were my parents, watching me, both looking a little frail, Mum dabbing a tear from her eye; on my right my pregnant wife was waiting at the door. It was a pivotal moment in my life. Mum handed me a tissue and I wiped the tears from my eyes; I hadn't realized I'd been crying. For once, my Dad didn't have a smart remark for me. "Good luck tonight, son," he said. Coming from my Dad, that was a Hallmark moment. Now my throat really tightened with love. I found myself unable to speak. A different man would have hugged his parents at that moment, but we never were a demonstrative bunch, so I nodded my head at them and blinked a few times.

I walked over to Cathy, and together we crossed the threshold of my parents' doorway, ready to face the concert that night and a new life together as parents. I felt as if I were finally leaving my youth behind. Only a couple of decades late. Cathy gripped my hand tightly—my God, that woman was strong when she was feeling emotional.

As we got into the car, I was thinking about how the Steven myth I'd created and worshipped in my mind all those years had evaporated. I breathed a massive sigh of relief—there was no Steven-god to worship or envy now, just an old friend who'd expressed an interest in seeing me over Christmas, a human being who'd devoted his life to helping others, not chasing fame and fortune as I had. He was a mere mortal, but now I really understood that there's nothing "mere" about any human life. *"Ya just don't get it, do ya?!"* I did now.

The irony of my columns wasn't lost on me—Steven really was a hero, doing his best to keep people alive in a dangerous part of the world. Deep down I perhaps may have sensed that all along, and so it had come out in the columns. It was a soothing possibility.

Steven was no longer a high school rockstar wannabee. He was a man, had been for a long time. And so was I: finally. I wasn't afraid any more. I was ready to rock as both a parent and a husband. Maybe Cathy and I would have three kids and we could teach them how to play instruments and we could travel around on a bus and become the next Partridge Family! But we'd call it the Love Family! Kind of like the Love Boat, but somehow connected with a family, and we could sell the idea to Hollywood and ... *Easy, Donny, easy.*

Deep breath. You're right, you're absolutely right ... Okay, so it wasn't going to be an instantaneous transformation into adulthood.

68.

8:00 p.m.

Showtime.

I was sitting in the darkened auditorium, praying intensely. *Maurice, please don't disappoint these people, please make this happen.*

The Irondale High School auditorium was humming. The place was smaller than I'd remembered, as is everything after you've grown up, but Sharon had made the best of a mediocre situation: she'd built a veritable arena concert set-up. The stage stretched the full width of the auditorium, hundreds of expensive lights and speakers hanging from scaffolds wreathing the stage. Dry ice flowed along the stage from beyond the drum riser. At the back of the stage hung a billboard-sized video screen. At the back in the balcony, where, as a student, I'd worked on the stage crew with the rest of the nerds, professional techies were manning spotlights and the sound board.

I was almost shaking with excitement and dread. Cathy grinned at me in the darkness, eyes huge with child-like anticipation.

A pungent wreath of pot smoke hung above the crowd. I watched a group of balding men two rows ahead of me passing a mickey along. It was like being at a Rolling Stones concert. The gorilla-sized security force fronting the stage didn't seem to mind the booze and pot; like everyone else, they were in high spirits. I nervously scanned the crowd. I spotted my old English teacher, Mr. Philips, six rows in front of us, with a girl who was probably his granddaughter riding his shoulders. He'd awarded Steven with the Grade 12 English Award—he'd been a big fan of Steven's poetry.

Earlier, outside the school, the parking lot and all of the neighbouring residential streets had been packed. Cathy and I had found ourselves walking through a throng of rock'n'roll tailgate partiers—people of all ages drinking, sharing weed, some on the football field even cooking up burgers and chicken on Hibachi barbecues.

"Donny Love!" a middle-aged guy had cried out, raising a beer. "What's up buddy?" He'd held out a hand to shake mine. At first I didn't recognize him. But under the layers of change, I soon recognized Tom Fitch, a jock I'd come to hate back in the day, and with him were Rob Woodley and Dave Rinehart, two more bully bastards. After Grade 8, when they'd hit puberty but I'd been relegated to the land of skinny, pimple-faced pariahs, their contempt and arrogance had filled me with toxic rage. I stared at this man, a stranger to me now, a different person from that young jerk. My anger shifted deep inside me, rolled over and went back to sleep. Tom was smiling and laughing, apparently unaware that he had ever had any negative impact on anyone. I felt a flooding sense of relief, knowing that I could leave my teen angst behind me for good. Tom's friendliness had erased the past in a single gesture. What power there was in goodwill!

Standing by his Volvo station wagon, we exchanged small talk and introduced each other to our wives. Tom had a booster seat and an infant carrier in the back seat. I caught Cathy looking wistfully at the Big Bird sun shade on the window, and we exchanged a potent smile.

We made our excuses and headed towards the school.

"Wow—how nice for you to meet up with on old friend," Cathy enthused.

I laughed. "That guy was the biggest bastard who ever walked the halls of Irondale," I said. "And he made my life hell for awhile, too."

Cathy looked perplexed. "He's not your friend? You just seemed to like each other."

"Water under the bridge, baby. You're looking at a guy who can leave the past where it belongs." Feeling cocky, I gave her bum a little grab.

"Donny!" she hissed, grinning. Her eyes darted around to see if anyone had noticed.

We waded through the crowds. Cathy had begged to go backstage, but I refused. I wanted to watch Maurice the Maestro perform his brilliant Steven McCartney impersonation from a safe distance. Running distance from the exits. I promised Cath that, if the show didn't completely stink and the crowds decided not to lynch me, we'd go backstage afterward. And that, yes, I would try to introduce her to Brad Pitt. Butterflies danced in my gut.

And Brad was there. Seriously. And a few other celebs who had obviously decided not to miss the photo ops. Flashes were going off everywhere, and the shrill shrieks of young women were making my eardrums bleed. Sharon had set up a red carpet and cordoned off a number of front row seats for the Hollywood crowd. Various bodyguards and security people stonily flanked their charges.

We'd quickly ducked into the last row and found some seats in the middle. I felt relieved no one had noticed us. Everyone was too busy gawping at Pam Anderson, who had tottered in on five-inch stilettos, wearing almost nothing. As we squeezed past a *Hollywood Tonight* reporter, I overheard her announcing to her audience that, unfortunately, Sir Paul McCartney was unable to make it to the show tonight. Apparently, he had been mildly injured by a prosthetic leg during a domestic assault with his soon-to-be ex wife.

Occasionally voices from the past greeted me: "Donny Love!" "How's it going?", "Let's talk after the show, man", "Man, where the hell have you been all these years?" and so on. I waved haphazardly, as hysteria had me firmly in its grip, almost numbing me into a stupor. I just couldn't focus on anything or anyone. *Start the show, let's go, let's go!*

Like Victor Frankenstein, my column had pieced together, limb by limb, a living, breathing monster. But it was a rather cool monster, I had to admit. Concert of the Century. People hooted and hollered and whistled. Butterflies the size of cats pounced in my belly now. I didn't want Maurice to disappoint these people. They wanted to see Steven, maybe some even needed to see Steven, to help them re-discover some lost magic. *Please Maurice, please make this happen.* I took Cathy's hand and squeezed.

The lights went out.

Darkness blanketed the auditorium.

I stopped breathing. "Shout", the song made famous by Tears for Fears, suddenly erupted through the speakers. The swelling crowd cheered shrilly, singing along, pumping their fists in the air.

The huge video screen came to life, Maurice silhouetted from behind—the lone gunslinger—the same image that Sharon had placed as a full-page layout in the *Gazette*. It was the image of a rock'n'roll god. The hairs rose on the nape of my neck.

The crowd roared.

Blinding lights lit up the darkness. Like a microphone-wielding ninja, Maurice flew onto center stage in a scissor kick, his hair flying, and the band kicked it off with "Sex Machine." Maurice was transformed. He wore a brilliant blue tailcoat, like a psychedelic ringmaster, and he now had a mane of wild, dark blonde curls. Tight black leather pants and purple jackboots completed the ensemble. He was definitely still wearing make-up, but there was nothing poncey about it. He was electric. He *was* a sex machine! As he strutted and jived, the crowd erupted.

And then, when he sang, my jaw dropped. He sounded just like James Brown, note for note, every nuance and inflection. I couldn't believe it. People all around us were on their feet, dancing. Cathy nudged me in the side, motioning with her head to start boogeying with her. I did, and I *really* got into it. I had been so pent-up for such a long time that I let it all hang out, every last molecule, and it felt cathartic.

In every number, Maurice was brilliant. In fact, I'd even say he was pure *genius*. I knew then that Steven couldn't have done this, not even in his heyday. Maurice was the real thing. He was in the realm of the greats, the Freddy Mercurys, the Elvises. He deserved to be a superstar!

He stormed through a non-stop set of Billy Idol Generation X material, having changed into a ripped white t-shirt and black stovepipe jeans, pumping his red Converse hightops with boundless energy and stabbing surprisingly well-muscled arms in the air. The 20-year-old beside

Cathy shrieked out "Steven, we love you!" after one number. Without missing a beat, Maurice called back, "Sweetheart, we love you, too!" Chameleon-like, he transformed his voice and appearance throughout the program, which included The English Beat, old Michael Jackson, the Beatles. I saw Mum and Dad slow-dancing in the front row to the Beatles "All You Need Is Love", Dad good-naturedly giving Maurice the finger behind Mum's back. Maurice cheerfully responded by bringing my folks up on stage to finish their dance. Not even my smartass Dad had the nerve to give him the finger on-stage.

Plaid pants held up by suspenders, and wearing his purple jackboots and a Brady Bunch T-shirt, Maurice even paid a tribute to Hamilton's greatest punk band, Teenage Head, by singing a revved-up version of "Picture My Face." Midway through the program, he proved himself to have a powerful talent for ballads, singing Burt Bacharach's "Going Out of My Head" with such ache in his voice that Cathy and I both started to tear up. A few lighters popped up into the air around us. And, God bless that big ham, he came out as Clint Eastwood, poncho and all, cigarello hanging from his lips, for a quirky rendition of the theme from the movie, *The Good, The Bad, and The Ugly*. The crowd loved that one.

There was a heart-stopping moment when I thought that the gig was up. In response to the non-stop shouting of his name by one determined girl, he raised his eyebrow suggestively and purred "Call me Maurrrrrice, you saucy little thing!", and then swung his leather-clad bum in her direction and smacked it a couple of times. The audience did not seem to be confused by this directive at all. In fact, more than a few voices called out the name "Maurice!" throughout the rest of the show. The suggestion of an alter-ego just excited the crowd more. They don't care what he calls himself, I thought in wonder. Maybe he doesn't even have to be Steven McCartney any more. I might just be off the hook here!

Maurice really worked over the audience. He pumped up the guys. He seduced the women. He had people crying and cheering and singing along. By the time he got to his final number, I think that we all felt deliciously pummelled. He sat down to a piano and the lighting became muted and magical. Sitting with quiet grace at the piano, he finished with an original song. A backdrop of stars and planets soared past behind him on the big video screen. As he sang the chorus "And you and I / are on this journey / together", you could feel the love in the hall.

They called him back for three ovations. And he ended up giving them all another 45 minutes of musical heaven.

At the end of the third encore, a loud slurry voice called out from the audience. "Steven, don't leave us, man!" There was a chorus of agreement from the crowd.

I felt my elation start to slip away. But Maurice neatly took possession of the ball.

"Is there anyone else here who would like to hear me sing another concert?" The crowd erupted enthusiastically. "Well, then, I'll just have to change my plans, won't I?"

At that moment I decided to leave the Steven legend in Maurice's hands. He could decide what was going to happen next. I was done. And, clearly, he could handle it better than I could.

As the house lights came up, I had a good look around, no longer afraid to meet anyone's eyes. My co-workers had shown. Bob Chamberlain stood at the side of the stage, dressed to the nines, wearing a backstage pass *(how did he get one of those?)*, yakking it up with Bob Yates, a CKOC Oldies radio personality. Meg and the others were milling about, laughing and relaxed-looking. They all seemed to be having a good time.

I spotted two of my old teachers, Miss Radic, my music teacher, and Mr. Henderson, who had terrorized generations of Irondale kids with his threats of push-ups if you were late for Math class. I wondered if they would remember me, the classic underachiever.

Cathy and I squeezed our way toward the Stage Door entrance, which was packed with eager reporters and fans. Over their heads I could see Sharon and a huge bouncer carefully screening people who were desperate to get in to meet Maurice. Reingruber was enthusiastically flailing his arms in the air to get my attention. Clinging to him was the red-headed librarian, looking far too attractive for the likes of our Norbie. Tony and Angela were chatting with John. Cathy and I pushed our way through to them, with me carving a pathway ahead of Cathy's pregnant belly like an icebreaker. Sharon gestured to us impatiently.

"C'mon already! You're missing all the fun!" she yelled over the din.

Tony and John clapped me on the shoulder. "You did it, Love," Tony said. "Man, I can't believe how freaking good that show was! That guy is the real deal, Donny."

John was practically dancing with excitement. "That show was amazing! I think I had an out-of-body experience," he laughed.

Reingruber just nodded his head voicelessly, his eyes suspiciously moist-looking. Morag discreetly handed him a Kleenex. Wow, Norb has found himself a keeper, I thought.

Sharon grabbed me by the arm and dragged me toward the dressing rooms. "He's been asking for you since the show ended, and I think that he's going to have a hissy fit if he doesn't soon see you, so get in there!" She looked frazzled—and like she was enjoying every minute of it.

I stopped her for a moment and impulsively gave her a big hug. She endured it, the way people who don't get hugged much do.

"Sharon, I want to thank you for all of this, this—magic that you did here tonight. You saved my life. And I didn't really deserve your help, either. As far as I'm concerned, you're a bloody goddam genius at what you do. A talent."

She looked a bit embarrassed, but pleased, too. "It was a fucking good show, wasn't it?" she asked thoughtfully. "And I do know how to pick'em, don't I? I mean, just between you and me," she lowered her voice a bit, "I was starting to think that maybe he wasn't going to put out the goods, you know? I was contemplating keeping a packed bag by the stage door." She gave me a wry grin. "Anyway, c'mon. The Maestro awaits!"

Maurice was holding court in his dressing room, which was actually an old prop room that had been cleared out and decorated in his honour. The relaxed, indulgent expression on his face changed immediately to furrowed concern when I came in. Grabbing my hands earnestly, Maurice asked "Well? Did I do it? Did I channel him?" His eyes searched mine.

It was breath-taking that such a monumental talent could have such insecurity, could be asking *me*, of all people, for validation.

"Maurice, you are a god, and I worship you," I said, in semi-seriousness.

He blew out air in exasperation. "Dammit," he half-whispered, glancing around at the crowd of people in the room, "I'm not talking to one of these bootlickers, am I? I'm talking to *you*,

Donald Love, and I want a straight, brutally honest answer from you. Did I get Steven right or not?" He glared at me sternly, daring me to try a joke again.

I choked down a nervous impulse to giggle and told him the truth. He deserved it.

"You were better than Steven. You were what Steven would have liked to be. No, actually, you were what *I* wanted Steven to be. In my greatest dreams, Maurice. Thank you. You rebuilt my faith in big dreams tonight."

His tense face relaxed. He looked like a man who had rebuilt his own faith in big dreams, too. "Well, I couldn't have done it without your help. You're the man who knows Steven best." He looked sheepish when he asked, "Do you think that Steven might have made it to the show tonight? That maybe he was in the audience, in a disguise perhaps, checking up on his doppelganger?" I could hear the note of hopefulness in his voice.

"Well, you never know, Maurice. I mean, there were a lot of important people out there tonight, checking you out. So, you never know."

He beamed.

69.

Cathy did meet Brad Pitt. But not because of anything that her helpful husband arranged. No, Cathy was desperately trying to make it to the girls' washroom, with several pounds of baby lying on her full bladder, when she accidentally knocked over a man in front of her with her stomach. The man turned out to be "Brad", as she later frequently reminded me, and he was apparently the most wonderful, kind, down-to-earth guy, and shockingly good-looking in real life. Shockingly.

Norbert Reingruber married Morag the Librarian a few months after the concert. They had a Star Trek-themed civil ceremony at his new collectibles store, which had more floor space than my house. Cathy insisted that we adhere to the bride and groom's dress code. I was Spock. Need I say more?

Tony and Angela invested some savings in a car that he and another mechanic raced at Cayuga Speedway. I don't think that Angela was too happy about Tony driving at the track, but she put up with it. That's what people do for the ones they love.

John will never give up the restaurant, but he found a salsa class with a ratio of eight women to every guy, and he tells me that he wasn't really that far off the mark when he told us that day at Tim Hortons that salsa is basically sex on the dance floor. He really enjoys those classes.

Sharon is off to New York. Or is it L.A.? Maybe both. She sounds pissed off when she talks about it, because she says that she resents having to leave her home in The Hammer for "these morons" in "the industry". But the truth is that she is seriously being courted by some big-time players, several well-established singers looking for new management, and at least one big movie studio looking for "fresh creative blood", and they are not sparing the expense in their offers to her. The next time I try to call her, I will probably have to go through two secretaries and a personal assistant.

70.

Now I don't have to tell you what happened to Maurice. You and every household in North America, the UK and Asia know him by name. The world had no time for anger over his Steven alias. As we speak, he's currently on the fourth month of a two-year run tearing up concert stadiums across the globe. He dedicates his shows to Steven. He told me that he always leaves a pass at the box office for Steven McCartney. Just in case he decides to show up.

Hey, a guy's gotta have a dream, right?

71.

Excerpt From
Donny Love's "In Town" Column

Saturday night I took my son Stewart to Copps Colliseum to see one of my favourite entertainers—Pam Anderson.

You may not be aware that Ms. Anderson is multi-talented. Perhaps you only know her as a Baywatch babe, bouncing down the beach to save some lucky guy's life. Perhaps you only know her as the bikini-clad bride of several of rock's bad boys. Perhaps you would only recognize her for her much-famed bosom.

Well, guess what? Pam Anderson is going to give Sharon, Lois, and Bram a run for their money. Her recently-released children's CD, *Pam's Magical Animal Kingdom*, has been topping the charts in children's entertainment. In interviews, Ms. Anderson said that she is ready for a new stage in her career and wants to leave her sex-kitten image behind.

I'm happy to say that she did not leave her sex-kitten clothing behind. Her stop in Hamilton, in the middle of her

North American tour, was sold out, and for good reason.

Stewart has been obsessively listening to Pam's CD, ever since his Uncle Norbert gave him the CD for Christmas. I just like looking at the cover. Stewart's mother keeps threatening to throw it in the garbage.

Stewart is not alone. If the children at this concert are any indicator, Pam has a long, lucrative career ahead of her. The songs are surprisingly catchy and the lyrics are as pure as the driven snow. Her voice is light, but sweet—just right for children's music. The animal characters she has created are a hit with the kids.

As a final note, I believe that Ms. Anderson has created a new phenomenon with her tour. In homes all over North America, fathers are begging to be the ones to take their tots to this children's show. The moms are happy, for once, to be left at home.